गणपत्युपनिषद्

Gaṇapati Upaniṣad

Rediscovering Indian Literary Classics
(ISSN - 0972-0111)

Rediscovering Indian Literary Classics, no. 13

अथर्वणवेदीया
गणपत्युपनिषद्

Gaṇapati Upaniṣad

With the Commentary Tattvaprakāśikā

by

Swami Tattvavidananda Saraswati

D.K. Printworld (P) Ltd.
New Delhi

Cataloging in Publication Data — DK

[Courtesy: D.K. Agencies (P) Ltd. <docinfo@dkagencies.com>]

Tattvavidananda Saraswati, *Swami,* 1948-
    Gaṇapati Upaniṣad : with the commentary
Tattvaprakāśikā = Atharvaṇavedīyā Gaṇapatyupaniṣad/
Swami Tattvavidananda Saraswati.
    x, 94 p. 22 cm.
    (Rediscovering Indian literary classics ; no. 13)
    Includes Index.
    ISBN 8124602654

    1. Upanishads. Gaṇapatyupaniṣad — Criticism.
interpretation, etc. I. Upanishads. Gaṇapatyupaniṣad.
English & Sanskrit. II. Title. III. Title: Atharvaṇavedīyā
Gaṇapatyupaniṣad. IV. Series: Rediscovering Indian
literary classics ; no. 13.

DDC 294.592 18   21

ISBN 81-246-0265-4
First Published in India in 2004
Second revised edition in 2006
© Author

All rights reserved. No part of this publication may be reproduced
or transmitted, except brief quotations, in any form or by any means,
electronic or mechanical, including photocopying, recording, or any
information storage or retrieval system, without prior written
permission of the copyright holder, indicated above, and the
publishers.

Published and printed by:
D.K. Printworld (P) Ltd.
Regd. office : '*Sri Kunj*', F-52, Bali Nagar
New Delhi - 110 015
Phones : (011) 2545-3975; 2546-6019; *Fax* : (011) 2546-5926
E-mail: dkprintworld@vsnl.net
Web: www.dkprintworld.com

Cataloging in Publication Data — DK

[Courtesy: D.K. Agencies (P) Ltd. <docinfo@dkagencies.com>]

**Dedicated
to
the Lord of Kailāsa**

Preface

MY family's association with Pujyasri Swami Dayananda Saraswati goes back a number of years and it was, therefore, natural for me to seek out the Arsha Vadya Gurukulam when we moved to New Jersey. It was in the hallowed precincts of the Gurukulam that we had the good fortune to listen to Sri Swami Tattvavidanandaji unfold Vedanta for the first time.

Sri Swami Tattvavidanandaji is one of Pujya Swami Dayananda Saraswati's foremost disciples, and one of the most authoritative exponents of Vadanta. We can abserve the grace with which he conducts himself, and the obvious *guru śaraddhā* that pervades his attitude. Sri Swami Tattvavidanandaji's use of simple language engages all levels of learners and his obvious mastery of the subject shines through in his teaching. We have all grown to enjoy his erudition, and learning from him is a memorable experience.

Sri Swami Tattvavidanandaji unfolded the meaning of the Gaṇapati Upaniṣad over the course of three lectures in New Jersey, in early 2002. At the end of each teaching session, Sri Swamiji patiently clarified doubts on a wide range of topics related to Vedanta.

Working with Sri Swami Tattvavidanandaji's lectures proved to be a wonderful way to revisit every word of his explanation of the text, and dwell upon each concept that he has so brilliantly explored. The exactitude of Sri Swamiji's language as he demystified esoteric concepts opened up a fascinating new world of Vedantic thought. I consider the time that I spent transcribing and editing this manuscript to be the period of my true introduction to Vedanta. I am grateful to Sri Swami Tattvavidanandaji for this valuable initiation.

In this book, Sri Swami Tattvavidanandaji carefully examines every line of the Gaṇapati Upaniṣad and gives extensive cross references with respect to meaning and usage that enable the reader to appreciate the beauty of the text. He also explores the derivative roots of many words that occur in the text so that the concepts may be understood better.

Sri Swami Tattvavidanandaji wishes to acknowledge, particularly, the contributions of Sri Mohan Bhujle of Holmdel, New Jersey, and Sri Puppal B. of Brahma Vidya Kuteer, Secunderabad, A.P., India, for their scholarly examination of this manuscript. Their invaluable comments and suggestions have greatly enhanced the value of this book.

Sri Swami Tattvavidanandaji and I would like to thank Sri Krishnakumar (KK) S. Davey of Livingston, New Jersey. It is his painstaking endeavour to make lectures such as these and other important teachings more widely available through publication. Our thanks also to Smt. Bindu Bhatt of Old Bridge, new Jersey for help with the publication of this and other books.

Warren, New Jersey   **Jayshree Ramakrishnan**
January, 2006

Key to Transliteration

VOWELS

अ *a*	आ *ā*	इ *i*	ई *ī*	उ *u*	ऊ *ū*
(b<u>u</u>t)	(p<u>a</u>lm)	(<u>i</u>t)	(b<u>ee</u>t)	(p<u>u</u>t)	(p<u>oo</u>l)
ऋ *ṛ*	ए *e*	ऐ *ai*	ओ *o*	औ *au*	
(<u>rhy</u>thm)	(pla<u>y</u>)	(<u>ai</u>r)	(t<u>oe</u>)	(l<u>ou</u>d)	

CONSONANTS

Guttural	क *ka*	ख* *kha*	ग *ga*	घ *gha*	ङ· *ṅa*
	(s<u>k</u>ate)	(bloc<u>kh</u>ead)	(<u>g</u>ate)	(<u>gh</u>ost)	(si<u>ng</u>)
Palatal	च *ca*	छ* *cha*	ज *ja*	झ *jha*	ञ *ña*
	(<u>ch</u>unk)	(cat<u>ch h</u>im)	(<u>j</u>ohn)	(he<u>dgeh</u>og)	(bu<u>nch</u>)
Cerebral	ट *ṭa*	ठ* *ṭha*	ड *ḍa*	ढ* *ḍha*	ण* *ṇa*
	(s<u>t</u>art)	(an<u>th</u>ill)	(<u>d</u>art)	(go<u>dh</u>ead)	(u<u>n</u>der)
Dental	त *ta*	थ *tha*	द *da*	ध* *dha*	न *na*
	(pa<u>th</u>)	(<u>th</u>under)	(<u>th</u>at)	(brea<u>the</u>)	(<u>n</u>umb)
Labial	प *pa*	फ* *pha*	ब *ba*	भ *bha*	म *ma*
	(s<u>p</u>in)	(<u>ph</u>iloso<u>ph</u>y)	(<u>b</u>in)	(a<u>bh</u>or)	(<u>m</u>uch)
Semi-vowels	य *ya*	र *ra*	ल *la*	व *va*	
	(<u>y</u>oung)	(d<u>r</u>ama)	(<u>l</u>uck)	(<u>v</u>ile)	
Sibilants	श *śa*	ष *ṣa*	स *sa*	ह *ha*	
	(<u>sh</u>ove)	(bu<u>sh</u>el)	(<u>s</u>o)	(<u>h</u>um)	
Others	क्ष *kṣa*	त्र *tra*	ज्ञ *jña*	ळ* *ḷ*	ऋ* *ṝ*
	(<u>kṣ</u>atriya)	(<u>tri</u>śūla)	(<u>jñā</u>ni)	(p<u>lay</u>)	

अं (⁻)ṁ *anusvāra* (nasalisation of preceding vowel) like *saṁskṛti*

अः *visarga* = *ḥ* (aspiration of preceding vowel) like (*prātaḥ*)

ऽ *Avagraha* consonant #'consonant (like:- *ime 'vasthitā*)

Anusvāra at the end of a line is presented by m (म्) and not ṁ

* No exact English equivalents for these letters.

Key to Transliteration

VOWELS

CONSONANTS

श्रीगणेशाय नमः

गणपत्युपनिषद्

Gaṇapati Upaniṣad
Text and
Commentary *Tattvaprakāśikā*

The Text

ओम्, भद्रं कर्णेभिः शृणुयाम देवाः। भद्रं पश्येमाक्षभिर्यजत्राः।
स्थिरैरङ्गैस्तुष्टुवाग्ंसस्तनूभिः। व्यशेम देवहितं यदायुः। स्वस्ति न इन्द्रो
वृद्धश्रवाः। स्वस्ति नः पूषा विश्ववेदाः। स्वस्ति नस्ताक्ष्यो अरिष्टनेमिः।
स्वस्ति नो बृहस्पतिर्दधातु। ओम्, शान्तिः शान्तिः शान्तिः।।

*om, bhadram karṇebhih śṛṇuyāma devāḥ। bhadram
paśyemākṣabhiryajatrāḥ। sthirairaṅgaistuṣṭuvāṁsastanūbhiḥ । vyaśema devahitam yadāyuḥ । svasti na
indro vṛddhaśravāḥ । svasti naḥ pūṣā viśvavedāḥ ।
svasti nastārkṣyo ariṣṭanemiḥ । svasti no bṛhaspatirdadhātu । oṁ śāntiḥ śāntiḥ śāntiḥ ॥*

ओं नमस्ते गणपतये ॥ १ ॥

oṁ namaste gaṇapataye ॥ 1 ॥

त्वमेव प्रत्यक्षं तत्त्वमसि। त्वमेव केवलं कर्तासि। त्वमेव केवलं धर्तासि।
त्वमेव केवलं हर्तासि। त्वमेव सर्वं खल्विदं ब्रह्मासि। त्वं साक्षादात्मासि
नित्यम् ॥ २ ॥

*tvameva pratyakṣaṁ tattvamasi। tvameva kevalaṁ
kartā'si। tvameva kevalaṁ dhartā'si। tvameva kevalaṁ
hartā'si। tvameva sarvaṁ khalvidaṁ brahmāsi। tvaṁ
sākṣādātmā'si nityam॥ 2 ॥*

ऋतं वच्मि । सत्यं वच्मि ।। ३ ।।

ṛtaṁ vacmi। satyaṁ vacmi।। 3 ।।

अव त्वं माम्। अव वक्तारम्। अव श्रोतारम्। अव दातारम्। अव धातारम्।
अवानूचानमव शिष्यम्। अव पुरस्तात्। अव दक्षिणात्तात्। अव पश्चात्तात्।
अवोत्तरात्तात्। अव चोध्वर्त्तात्। अवाधरात्तात्। सर्वतो मां पाहि पाहि
समन्तात्।। ४।।

*ava tvaṁ mām। ava vaktāram। ava śrotāram। ava
dātāram। ava dhātāram। avānūcānamava śiṣyam।
ava purastāt। ava dakṣiṇāttāt। ava paścāttāt।
avottarāttāt। ava cordhvāttāt। avādharāttāt। sarvato
māṁ pāhi pāhi samantāt।। 4 ।।*

त्वं वाङ्मयस्त्वं चिन्मयः। त्वमानन्दमयस्त्वं ब्रह्ममयः। त्वं
सच्चिदानन्दाऽद्वितीयोऽसि। त्वं प्रत्यक्षं ब्रह्मासि। त्वं ज्ञानमयो विज्ञानमयोऽसि
।। ५ ।।

*tvaṁ vāṅmayastvaṁ cinmayaḥ। tvamānanda-
mayastvaṁ brahmamayaḥ। tvaṁ saccidānandā'
dvitīyo'si। tvaṁ pratyakṣaṁ brahmāsi। tvaṁ
jñānamayo vijñānamayo'si।। 5 ।।*

सर्वं जगदिदं त्वत्तो जायते। सर्वं जगदिदं त्वत्तस्तिष्ठति। सर्वं जगदिदं त्वयि
लयमेष्यति। सर्वं जगदिदं त्वयि प्रत्येति। त्वं भूमिरापोऽनलोऽनिलो नभः।
त्वं चत्वारि वाक् (परिमिता) पदानि। त्वं गुणत्रयातीतः। त्वं अवस्थात्रयातीतः।
त्वं देहत्रयातीतः। त्वं कालत्रयातीतः। त्वं मूलाधारस्थितोऽसि नित्यम्। त्वं
शक्तित्रयात्मकः। त्वां योगिनो ध्यायन्ति नित्यम्। त्वं ब्रह्मा त्वं विष्णुस्त्वं
रुद्रस्त्वमिन्द्रस्त्वमग्निस्त्वं वायुस्त्वं सूर्यस्त्वं चन्द्रमास्त्वं ब्रह्म भूर्भुवस्सुवरोम्
।। ६ ।।

sarvaṁ jagadidaṁ tvatto jāyate ǀ sarvaṁ jagadidaṁ tvattastiṣṭhati ǀ sarvaṁ jagadidaṁ tvayi layameṣyati ǀ sarvaṁ jagadidaṁ tvayi pratyeti ǀ tvaṁ bhūmi-rāpo'nalo'nilo nabhaḥ ǀ tvaṁ catvāri vāk (parimitā) padāni ǀ tvaṁ guṇatrayātītaḥ ǀ tvaṁ avasthātrayātītaḥ ǀ tvaṁ dehatrayātītaḥ ǀ tvaṁ kālatrayātītaḥ ǀ tvaṁ mūlādhārasthito'si nityam ǀ tvaṁ śaktitrayātmakaḥ ǀ tvāṁ yogino dhyāyanti nityam ǀ tvaṁ brahmā tvaṁ viṣṇustvaṁ rudrastvamindrastvamagnistvaṁ vāyu-stvaṁ sūryastvaṁ candramāstvaṁ brahma bhūrbhu-vassuvarom ǁ 6 ǁ

गणादिं पूर्वमुच्चार्य वर्णादींस्तदनन्तरम् ǀ अनुस्वारः परतरः ǀ अर्धेन्दुलसितम् ǀ तारेण ऋद्धम् ǀ एतत्तव मनुस्वरूपम् ǁ ७ ǁ

gaṇādiṁ pūrvamuccārya varṇādīṁstadanantaram ǀ anusvāraḥ parataraḥ ǀ ardhendulasitam ǀ tāreṇa ṛddham ǀ etattava manusvarūpam ǁ 7 ǁ

गकारः पूर्वरूपम् ǀ अकारो मध्यमरूपम् ǀ अनुस्वारश्चान्त्यरूपम् ǀ बिन्दुरुत्तररूपम् ǀ नादस्संधानम् ǀ सगुंहिता संधिः ǁ ८ ǁ

gakāraḥ pūrvarūpam ǀ akāro madhyamarūpam ǀ anusvāraścāntyarūpam ǀ binduruttararūpam ǀ nāda-ssandhānam ǀ saguṁhitā sandhiḥ ǁ 8 ǁ

सैषा गणेशविद्या ǀ गणक ऋषिः ǀ निचृद्गायत्रीच्छन्दः ǀ गणपतिर्देवता ǀ ओम् गं गणपतये नमः ǁ ९ ǁ

saiṣā gaṇeśavidyā ǀ gaṇaka ṛṣiḥ ǀ nicṛdgāyatrīcchandaḥ ǀ gaṇapatirdevatā ǀ oṁ gaṁ gaṇapataye namaḥ ǁ 9 ǁ

एकदन्ताय विद्महे वक्रतुण्डाय धीमहि। तन्नो दन्तिः प्रचोदयात्।।

ekadantāya vidmahe vakratuṇḍāya dhīmahi। tanno
dantiḥ pracodayāt।। 10 ।।

एकदन्तं चतुर्हस्तं पाशमङ्कुशधारिणम्। रदं च वरदं हस्तैर्बिभ्राणं मूषकध्वजम्।।
रक्तं लम्बोदरं शूर्पकर्णकं रक्तवाससम्। रक्तगन्धानुलिप्ताङ्गं
रक्तपुष्पैस्सुपूजितम्।। भक्तानुकम्पिनं देवं जगत्कारणमच्युतम्। आविर्भूतं
च सृष्ट्यादौ प्रकृतेः पुरुषात्परम्। एवं ध्यायति यो नित्यं स योगी योगिनां
वरः ।। ११ ।।

ekadantaṁ caturhastaṁ pāśamaṅkuśadhāriṇam।
radaṁ ca varadaṁ hastairbibhrāṇaṁ mūṣakadhvajam।
raktaṁ lambodaraṁ śūrpakarṇakaṁ raktavāsasam।
raktagandhānuliptāṅgaṁ raktapuṣpaissupūjitam।
bhaktānukampinaṁ devaṁ jagatkāraṇamacyutam।
āvirbhūtaṁ ca sṛṣṭyādau prakṛteḥ puruṣātparam। evaṁ
dhyāyati yo nityaṁ sa yogī yogināṁ varaḥ।। 11 ।।

नमो व्रातपतये। नमो गणपतये। नमः प्रमथपतये। नमस्तेऽस्तु
लम्बोदरायैकदन्ताय विघ्ननाशिने शिवसुताय वरदमूर्तये नमः।। १२

namo vrātapataye। namo gaṇapataye। namaḥ
pramathapataye। namaste'stu lambodarāyaikadantāya
vighnanāśine śivasutāya varadamūrtaye namaḥ।। 12 ।।

एतदथर्वशीर्षं योऽधीते स ब्रह्मभूयाय कल्पते। स सर्वविघ्नैर्न बाध्यते। स
सर्वत्र सुखमेधते। स पञ्चमहापापात्प्रमुच्यते। सायमधीयानो दिवसकृतं
पापं नाशयति। प्रातरधीयानो रात्रिकृतं पापं नाशयति। सायं प्रातः प्रयुञ्जानो
पापोऽपापो भवति। सर्वत्राधीयानोऽपविघ्नो भवति। धर्मार्थकाममोक्षं च
विन्दते ।। १३ ।।

etadatharvaśīrṣaṁ yo'dhīte sa brahmabhūyāya kalpate । sa sarvavighnairna bādhyate । sa sarvatra sukhamedhate । sa pañcamahāpāpātpramucyate । sāyamadhīyāno divasakṛtaṁ pāpaṁ nāśayati । prātaradhīyāno rātrikṛtaṁ pāpaṁ nāśayati । sāyaṁ prātaḥ prayuñjāno pāpo'pāpo bhavati । sarvatrādhīyāno'-pavighno bhavati । dharmārtha-kāmamokṣaṁ ca vindate ॥ 13 ॥

इदमथर्वशीर्षमशिष्याय न देयम्। यो यदि मोहाद्दास्यति स पापीयान् भवति। सहस्रावर्तनाद्यं यं काममधीते तं तमनेन साधयेत् ।।१४।।

idamatharvaśīrṣamaśiṣyāya na deyam । yo yadi mohāddāsyati sa pāpīyān bhavati । sahasrāvartanādyaṁ yaṁ kāmamadhīte taṁ tamanena sādhayet ॥ 14 ॥

अनेन गणपतिमभिषिञ्चति स वाग्मी भवति। चतुर्थ्यामनश्नन् जपति स विद्यावान् भवति। इत्यथर्वणवाक्यम्। ब्रह्माद्यावरणं विद्यान्न बिभेति कदाचनेति ।। १५ ।।

anena gaṇapatimabhiṣiñcati sa vāgmī bhavati । caturthyāmanaśnan japati sa vidyāvān bhavati । ityatharvaṇavākyam । brahmādyāvaraṇaṁ vidyānna bibheti kadācaneti ॥ 15 ॥

यो दूर्वाङ्कुरैर्यजति स वैश्रवणोपमो भवति। यो लाजैर्यजति स यशोवान् भवति। स मेधावान् भवति। यो मोदकंसहस्रेण यजति स वाञ्छितफलमवाप्नोति। यस्साज्यसमिद्भिर्यजति स सर्वं लभते स सर्वं लभते ।। १६ ।।

yo dūrvāṅkurairyajati sa vaiśravaṇopamo bhavati। *yo
lājairyajati sa yaśovān bhavati*। *sa medhāvān bhavati*।
*yo modakasahasreṇa yajati sa vāñchitaphalamavāp-
noti*। *yassājyasamidbhiryajati sa sarvaṁ labhate sa
sarvaṁ labhate*।। 16 ।।

अष्टौ ब्राह्मणान् सम्यग् ग्राहयित्वा सूर्यवर्चस्वी भवति। सूर्यग्रहे महानद्यां
प्रतिमासन्निधौ वा जप्त्वा सिद्धमन्त्रो भवति। महाविघ्नात् प्रमुच्यते। महादोषात्
प्रमुच्यते। महाप्रत्यवायात् प्रमुच्यते। स सर्वविद्भवति स सर्वविद्भवति। य
एवं वेद। इत्युपनिषत् ।।१७।।

ॐ शान्तिश्शान्तिश्शान्तिः ।।

*aṣṭau brāhmaṇān samyag grāhayitvā sūryavarcasvī
bhavati*। *sūryagrahe mahānadyāṁ pratimāsannidhau
vā japtvā siddhamantro bhavati*। *mahāvighnāt
pramucyate*। *mahādoṣāt pramucyate*। *mahāpratyavāyāt
pramucyate*। *sa sarvavidbhavati sa sarvavidbhavati*।
ya evaṁ veda। *ityupaniṣat*।। 17 ।।

oṁ śāntiśśāntiśśāntiḥ.

।। हरिः ओम्, तत्सत्, श्रीकृष्णार्पणमस्तु ।।

।। *hariḥ oṁ, tatsat, śrīkṛṣṇārpaṇamastu* ।।

✳ ✳ ✳ ✳ ✳

Commentary

THE *Gaṇapati Upaniṣad* is found in the concluding part of the *Atharvaveda*. Hence it is also called *Atharva śīrṣa*. The *Atharvaveda* is the most secular of the four Vedas, in that it deals with worldly matters and issues in the manner and to the extent not addressed by the other three Vedas: the *Ṛgveda*, the *Yajurveda* and the *Sāmaveda*; yet it contains some profound Upaniṣads. Atharvaṇa is the name of a *ṛṣi*, the seer.

न थर्वति चलति इति अथर्वण: ।

na tharvati, calati iti atharvaṇaḥ ।

The one who has no vacillation of the mind (who is steady in his vision) is called Atharvaṇa.

The entire Veda is called the *Atharvaveda* after him. Each Veda has its own Upaniṣads. To name just a few, the *Yajurveda* has many well-known Upaniṣads such as the *Taittirīya*, the *Bṛhadāraṇyaka* and the *Kaṭha*. The *Chāndogya* and the *Kena* Upaniṣads are part of the *Sāmaveda*. The *Aitareya Upaniṣad* is the contribution from the *Ṛgveda*. The *Atharvaveda* contains profound Upaniṣads such as the *Muṇḍaka*, the *Māṇḍūkya* and the *Praśna*. Śrī Śaṅkara provided excellent commentaries called *Bhāṣyas* for all these Upaniṣads.

There are ten major Upaniṣads. They are considered to be major because Śrī Śaṅkara wrote commentaries on them. All the other Upaniṣads are considered minor. One should not, therefore, infer that the terms "major" and "minor" refer to the size of the Upaniṣads. The *Gaṇapati Upaniṣad* is a minor Upaniṣad, only because Śrī Śaṅkara has not commented upon it. Upaniṣad Brahmayogī, the disciple of Vāsudevendra, embellished this Upaniṣad with a fine commentary.

There are many *upāsanā*s in the Upaniṣads. *Upāsanā*, the worship of *Īśvara*, is an important step in making progress towards the discovery of the final Truth, which is the oneness of the individual with Īśvara. The *Gaṇapati Upaniṣad* is an important Upaniṣad because it deals with *upāsanā* as well as it teaches the ultimate Reality, the *Sat-cit-ānanda para-Brahman*, in Which everything resolves.

Until one understands the Truth of the Self being the whole (*ātmā vā īdaṃ sarvam*), and learns that there is no second entity at all to fear, one lives a life fraught with insecurity. There is always a job to finish, a mission to accomplish, or a journey to complete. Human psychology is such that when we undertake an important project and proceed forward with determined effort, the emotional makeup of the mind projects insecurity straightaway. As a result, we naturally wish to pray for the successful completion of the project. That is when one relates with more devotion and fervour than usual to *Īśvara* who is particularly adept at eliminating obstacles from the chosen path of the devotee. The nature of *upāsanā* of *Īśvara* is indeed determined by the emotional content of the human mind. The particular form of *Īśvara*, which removes the obstacles when worshipped, is Gaṇeśa. Such an *upāsanā* with the recitation of this Upaniṣad is a very potent method of securing all the hidden variables of a project in our favour.

But the main purpose of the Upaniṣad is beyond securing a few mundane benefits. This *upāsanā* can help the seeker in purifying the mind, thus making him or her eligible for the realization of the ultimate Truth. The word Upaniṣad indeed means that knowledge which takes the individual closest to *Īśvara* by eliminating the ignorance of one's own true nature.

As usual, the Upaniṣad starts with a peace invocation:

ओम्, भद्रं कर्णेभिः शृणुयाम देवाः । भद्रं पश्येमाक्षभिर्यजत्राः । स्थिरैरङ्गैस्तुष्टुवाग्ंसस्तनूभिः । व्यशेम देवहितं यदायुः । स्वस्ति न इन्द्रो वृद्धश्रवाः । स्वस्ति नः पूषा विश्ववेदाः । स्वस्ति नस्तार्क्ष्यो अरिष्टनेमिः । स्वस्ति नो बृहस्पतिर्दधातु । ओम्, शान्तिः शान्तिः शान्तिः ।।

om, bhadraṁ karṇebhiḥ śṛṇuyāma devāḥ ι bhadraṁ paśyemākṣabhiryajatrāḥ ι sthirair-aṅgaistuṣṭuvāṁsastanūbhiḥ ι vyaśema deva-hitaṁ yadāyuḥ ι svasti na indro vṛddhaśravāḥ ι svasti naḥ pūṣā viśvavedāḥ ι svasti nastārkṣyo ariṣṭanemiḥ ι svasti no bṛhaspatirdadhātu ι oṁ śāntiḥ śāntiḥ śāntiḥ ιι

Om. O gods, may we listen to the auspicious sounds with the ears. May we become proficient in Vedic rituals and may we see the auspicious things with the eyes. May we have healthy bodies with strong limbs so that we may utilize our life-span extolling the glory of the gods and propitiating them. May the Lord Indra of immense fame, who inspires us to perform good actions, bring prosperity to us. May Pūṣan, the omniscient, bless us with the good things of life. May Garuḍa, the son of Kaśyapa, destroy the adversity like a discus (which obliterates the objects blocking its flight). May He bless us with auspicious things

in life. May the Lord Bṛhaspati bring us glory
in life. *Om.* Let there be cessation of suffering
of the body. Let there be cessation of suffering
from the elements. Let there be cessation of
suffering caused by gods.

Om is the most sacred syllable and is the foremost name
and symbol of *Īśvara*. All the Vedic chanting starts with *om*
and ends with *om.* The essence of its teaching is contained
in *om.* It is also the primordial sound of this universe. The
Vedas maintain that this universe originated from the sound
om. It is the hypothesis of modern cosmologists subscribing
to the "Big Bang" theory that at the time of creation there
was a sound of big explosion of the primordial ylem from
which the universe came forth. This sound is *om.*

Description of the glory of *om*, in some detail, can be
found in the *Kaṭhopaniṣad* :

सर्वे वेदा यत्पदमामनन्ति तपांसि सर्वाणि च यद्वदन्ति । यदिच्छन्तो ब्रह्मचर्यं
चरन्ति तत्ते पदं संग्रहेण ब्रवीम्योमित्येतत् ।। — १-२-१५

sarve vedā yatpadamāmananti tapāṁsi sarvāṇi ca
yadvadanti ı yadicchanto brahmacaryaṁ caranti tatte
padaṁ saṅgraheṇa bravīmyomityetat — 1-2-15

All the Vedas teach that the Supreme Reality,
Brahman as the ultimate goal is to be reached by the
seeker through *om.* All austerities are aimed at
(reaching) that Reality alone. To gain That, the
seekers pursue knowledge by the study of the Vedas.
That ultimate Truth is pointed out in the briefest
possible way by the sound *om.*

एतदालम्बनं श्रेष्ठमेतदालम्बनं परम् ।
एतदालम्बनं ज्ञात्वा यो यदिच्छति तस्य तत् ।। — १-२-१७

etadālambanaṁ   śreṣṭhametadālambanaṁ   param ।
etadālambanaṁ jñātvā yo yadicchati tasya tat — 1-2-17

This is the best among the supports (for the mind).
One may meditate on the *saguṇa Brahman* or one
may abide in *para-Brahman* with the help of *om*. So,
one gets what one wants with the help of *om*.

Om can serve as an anchor in meditation on the Personal
God (a specific form of the formless *Brahman* particularly
appealing to the mind of the devotee). The Personal God is
also referred to as the *saguṇa Brahman*. Instead, if the seeker
wants to contemplate on the attributeless formless (*nirguṇa
nirākāra*) *Brahman*, even then *Om* serves as the best support
for launching the wavering mind into the background
Awareness that is *Brahman*.

Yo yadicchati tasya tat. Om represents both the attributeless
Brahman as well as the Personal God. That is the reason
why *oṅkāra* becomes part and parcel of the lifestyle of a
seeker committed to rituals and duties. Similarly, *oṅkāra*
becomes an inseparable part of the routine of a renunciate
who renounces all duties in order to contemplate on the
attributeless *Brahman*, the Awareness Absolute.

Bhadraṁ karṇebhiḥ. This is a very interesting prayer. The
Vedic prayers have their own flavour. Purāṇic prayers also
have a distinct flavour. Many Vedic prayers including the
most famous *gāyatrī mantra* are community prayers recited
by devotees for the benefit of the whole community. For
example, take the following prayer from the *Kṛṣṇa Yajurveda
Taittirīya Saṁhitā* (7-5-18) :

आ ब्रह्मन् ब्राह्मणो ब्रह्मवर्चसी जायतामास्मिन् राष्ट्रे राजन्य इषव्यश्शूरो
महारथो जायतां दोग्ध्री धेनुः . . . पुरन्धिर्योषा . . . निकामे निकामे नः
पर्जन्यो वर्षतु फलिन्यो न ओषधयः पच्यन्तां योगक्षेमो नः कल्पताम् ।।

*ā brahman brāhmaṇo brahmavarcasī jāyatāmāsmin
rāṣṭre rājanya iṣavyaśśūro mahāratho jāyatām dogdhrī
dhenuḥ . . . purandhriryoṣā . . . nikāme nikāme naḥ
parjanyo varṣatu phalinyo na oṣadhayaḥ pacyantām
yōgakṣemo naḥ kalpatām* ॥

In this nation, may the intellectual gain all round
development in his academic pursuits. May the
warrior (ruling) class have the courage and strength
and means (to ward off the enemy and to give
benevolent governance to the people). May the
production of milk be plentiful. . . . May the women
of the community gain prosperity. May there be
copious, timely and beneficial rainfall during the
year. May the harvest of crops be plentiful. May we
all gain what we do not have and retain all the good
things of life that we already have.

This is a typical community prayer of the Vedas. The Vedas
also have prayers aimed at prosperity for the individual.

Devāḥ. O gods, is an address in the plural. There are a
number of gods, each representing a limb of the Universal
Person, the Godhead. The famous *Puruṣa Sūkta* of the
R̥gveda describes the glory of the Cosmic Person in great
detail. This physical universe is visualized and understood
as the physical body of the Cosmic Person. Such a
visualization is the basis for the *viśvarūpa upāsanā*
(meditating upon the Lord manifest in the form of the
universe), which is prescribed for the seekers in the twelfth
chapter of the *Gītā*.

The entire universe is nothing but the manifestation of
the Cosmic Power. Everything in this universe from an atom
or a subatomic particle to the very galaxies (*aṇoraṇīyān
mahato mahīyān*, smaller than the smallest and bigger than
the biggest) is a manifestation of the Cosmic Power. All

that we perceive as real is but a *līlā*, play of the Godhead wielding this Power. The reality of the universe is the Cosmic Power and the *Brahman* from which it originates.

We can liken this universe to the shadow of a person. The shadow is not real. The person alone is real. We take the shadow to be real only because it is related to the real. If it were not, the shadow would not be even perceived by anybody. Similarly, this shadow-like universe is in place and perceived as such, because it is ever related to the *Brahman* through the Cosmic Power, which itself is non-different from the *Brahman*.

We assume many things as real and absolute. We imagine that we are "doing" this or that. In the vision of the enlightened person there is no such "doing". There is only the non-dual *Brahman*. When a movie is screened in a theatre, the reality of the scenes seen on the lighted screen is nothing but light. The light has nothing to do with the motion perceived by the audience. The motion is illusory; it belongs to the film. The movie on the screen is perceived due to a rapid succession of one static image after another, there being no physical connection between the successive images. If I were to project one picture frame for a couple of minutes, turn the light off for another minute, and then project a second picture frame, turn the light off again, and so on, would you perceive the motion? Of course, not. Would the first frame be the motion, or the second frame, or the gap between the two ? None. In reality, there is no motion. However, if the same thing is done while allowing a gap of barely a microsecond between the successive picture frames, we would perceive a motion entirely due to the trick of the senses and the mind.

Similarly, the film-like mind accounts for the movement perceived by us in the form of the world. In reality, there is only the immovable background Awareness which is

Brahman. Motion is perceived in the light of memory, which connects the position of an object of the earlier moment with that of the present moment. The observation in the present moment when connected with the impression of the observation of the earlier moment stored in the memory gives an illusion of motion, which is false. Śrī Śaṅkara in his *Bhāṣya* on the *Gītā* (4-18) says:

वस्त्वप्राप्यैव हि सर्व एव क्रियाकारकादिफलव्यवहार अविद्याभूमावेव ।

vastvaprāpyaiva hi sarva eva kriyākārakādiphala-vyavahāra avidyābhūmāveva ।

All this paraphernalia of action, agent, instruments, etc., and the result thereof are only in the backdrop of ignorance, and only before one gains the Reality that is *Brahman* by knowledge.

Power has no name or form. When power manifests, it gains a name and form. For instance, a "fan," a "refrigerator" or a "heater" is a name and form of the manifestation of the electric power. Similarly when the infinite Cosmic Power manifests, it gains a name and form. Each of the innumerable aspects of this manifestation is called a *devatā*. The gods are all the manifestation of the One Cosmic Power. The word *deva* or *devatā* is derived from the root *div*, which means light or power. This light is two-fold. One is the visible or physical light, and the other is the light of consciousness in which everything including the physical light shines.

When we propitiate a god, we are, in fact, relating to one particular manifestation of the Cosmic Power. This vision of the Cosmic Power manifesting as many gods is very beautifully illustrated in a significant dailogue between the sages Śākalya and Yājñavalkya in the *Bṛhadāraṇyaka Upaniṣad* (3-9). The former asks: How many gods are there?

The latter answers: Three thousand three hundred and six. Prompted by Śākalya again and again, Yājñavalkya modifies this number to thirty-three, then to six, then three, then two and finally to one. These numbers are explained as follows. The gods are indeed thirty-three in number. The number three thousand and odd belongs to their manifold glories pervading the entire universe. Very interestingly, when India became independent, we were thirty-three crore people.

The break-up of the number thirty three is as follows. Eight Vasus, eleven Rudras, twelve Ādityas, Indra, and Prajāpati. The eight Vasus are earth, wind, fire, atmosphere, sun, heavens (interstellar space), moon, and stars. The five sense-organs, the five organs of action, and the mind of the individual (who represents the Cosmic Person at the micro-level) together are the eleven Rudras. The Vedic timescale has the year as the basic unit based on the motion of the sun. It is divided into twelve months, each of which is personified as a god, Āditya. The rain bearing clouds are personified as Indra, and the animal kingdom as a whole is Prajāpati.

This number thirty-three is then reduced to six. The six gods are fire, earth, wind, atmosphere, sun, and the heavens. These six are further reduced to three by merging the earth into the fire, the atmosphere into the wind, and the heavens into the Sun. These three gods are finally merged into the Cosmic Person called Hiraṇyagarbha, the name indicating that the Cosmic Person is indeed the personification of the Cosmic Power. Thus, It is the One in all and all in the One.

This being so, we cannot assume agency or doership of anything we do. If I walk, it is the play of the Cosmic Power. If I speak, it is again the Cosmic Power in action. Anything that I do is the manifestation of the Cosmic Power at the micro-level.

In the Vedic prayers, the devotee sometimes addresses the universal Cosmic Power itself. On certain other occasions, the devotee may address the *devatās*, the individual manifestations of the Cosmic Power. Let us consider one important *mantra* of the *Taittirīya Saṁhitā* (4-1-8) :

हिरण्यगर्भस्समवर्तताग्रे भूतस्य जातः पतिरेक आसीत् ।

स दाधार पृथिवीं द्यामुतेमां कस्मै देवाय हविषा विधेम ।।

hiraṇyagarbhassamavartatāgre bhūtasya jātaḥ patireka āsīt ।

sa dādhāra pṛthivīṁ dyāmutemāṁ kasmai devāya haviṣā vidhema ।।

At the beginning Hiraṇyagarbha manifested and eventually became the One Overlord of all the creation that manifested out of Himself. He held together this earth and the heavens. We propitiate that Lord, the sustainer of all life, by offering oblations.

This *mantra* has a question and the answer hidden in it, *kasmai devāya haviṣā vidhema*. The question is, "Which God do we propitiate with oblations ?" *Kasmai* means *ekasmai; e* is hidden. It means that we propitiate that one God with oblations; all the gods like Āditya, Indra, etc., are so many limbs of that one God, Hiraṇyagarbha, the Cosmic Power. It was there in the beginning, and now also It alone exists. This globe, planets, stars, galaxies, etc., are held in place by that universal Power.

Bhadraṁ karṇebhiḥ śṛṇuyāma devāḥ. This is a community prayer. *Karṇebhiḥ, karṇaih,* with the ears. Whatever we hear, may it be good and auspicious. When we listen to music, it should be good and auspicious. It should reduce the agitation of the mind and it should not be meaningless. It need not always be about God. It may refer to some noble human sentiment like compassion, and may be in any language, but it has to be auspicious. Elders should not use harsh and inappropriate language with children or youngsters, even when they get angry. Our speech should always be soft and moderate. No inauspicious word should ever be uttered or heard within the confines of home. Discussions or discourses about the Lord or *ātman* are the most auspicious.

Bhadraṁ paśyemākṣabhiryajatrāḥ. Yaja is worship of the Lord. It could be an elaborate Vedic ritual, or a simple act of prayer like *pūjā*. Yajatra is one who is proficient in such a worship. We should make such a worship a regular discipline, *nitya karma*, in our life. We should start the day with a prayer, lead the day with a prayerful attitude, and conclude the day yet again with a prayer. This kind of disposition of being prayerful all the time would be a wonderful solution to all problems and suffering. The worship of the Lord is not merely visiting places of worship. Lord Śrī Kṛṣṇa describes a superior kind of worship in the *Gītā* (18-46) as follows:

यतः प्रवृत्तिर्भूतानां येन सर्वमिदं ततम् ।
स्वकर्मणा तमभ्यर्च्य सिद्धिं विन्दति मानवः ॥

yataḥ pravṛttirbhūtānāṁ yena sarvamidaṁ tatam |
svakarmaṇā tamabhyarcya siddhiṁ vindati mānavaḥ ||

Everything in the creation has emanated from the Lord, and hence all this is pervaded by Him. Therefore, performing one's duty is the superior form of worshipping the Lord. By doing so, one becomes accomplished (in terms of gaining the purity of heart), and eligible for gaining Self-knowledge.

Therefore, all righteous actions including community service rendered with a worshipful attitude are indeed a

worship of the Lord. Here the prayer states that we may
see good and auspicious things with our eyes in this life.
From this we should not conclude that anything to do with
festivities alone is auspicious and the opposite is
inauspicious. Whatever is *dharma* or righteous is auspicious,
and whatever is *adharma* or unrighteous is inauspicious.
May we use our collective energy for a good purpose and
towards auspicious ends.

Sthirairaṅgaistuṣṭuvāṁsastanūbhiḥ. To be able to see good
things and hear good things, one should have good health.
When the person is healthy, the world appears good; he or
she is better able to enjoy the world. All enjoyment has its
basis in the healthy body. Even to perform good deeds, we
need robust health. In this regard, the following saying of
our national poet Kālidāsa from his poem *Kumārasambhava*
(5) is very popular among the students of Sanskrit:

शरीरमाद्यं खलु धर्मसाधनम् ।

śarīramādyaṁ khalu dharmasādhanam ।

Healthy body is the foremost means of performing
righteous actions.

Healthy body is one of the most important means to achieve
dharma, because *dharma* is nothing other than performing
righteous actions. One should be very cautious about the
sensual pleasures, because they consume the body. For
instance, while we enjoy eating good food, the body cannot
sustain the onslaught of rich food and elaborate meals. The
mind is insatiable. The body can never cope with the
demands of the mind. There is always that big gulf between
the body and the mind. One should safeguard one's health,
and the only way of doing so is through moderation.
Moderation is indeed *dharma*. Moderation should be our
watchword and we should practise it for lifetime. We should
keep sensual pleasures at a safe distance.

Tuṣṭuvāṁsaḥ, prayerful. We may start the day with a prayer and end it with a prayer. The entire day then gets sanctified by the prayer. Prayer is the one means that connects us with the Reality. A day without prayer means a day that has gone in the service of the unreal. A day that is started with prayer and concluded with another prayer connects the person with the Reality; even though in between, the person has been dealing with the unreal. Just as truth is its own reward, so also is prayer its own reward. Here prayer is to enable one to live this kind of prayerful life. In India, such a prayerful disposition is built into the culture of the land. In birth we pray; in death we pray; we pray in health and in sickness, in good times and in bad times. Even a beggar invokes the name of the Lord when he begs. We take the name of the Lord when we sneeze. After sitting cross-legged for some time, we get up taking the name of the Lord. The people are named after the Lord, so that we repeat the name of the Lord innumerable times a day without any conscious effort. But, we should be cautious not to make the whole prayer perfunctory. The prayerful disposition is sustained by intense love or feeling for the Lord, who is the only Reality of this universe.

Vyaśema devahitaṁ yadāyuḥ. The purpose of living is adequately served, when we lead our lives hearing good things, and seeing good things with a healthy body and a prayerful attitude. What we earn or achieve during each day is in the realm of *saṁsāra* and therefore, it is unreal. As we have seen earlier, like the person and his shadow, the achievements of each day seem real only through their connection with the Reality, which is *Īśvara*, while they are unreal by themselves. Therefore, the purpose of life is fulfilled by devotion to the Lord and by acquiring Self-knowledge.

Svasti na indro vṛddhaśravāḥ. The god Indra is highly eulogized in the *Ṛgveda*. A major portion of the *Ṛgveda* is dedicated to praising the glory of Indra. Therefore it is appropriately said that Indra is the most renowned of all the gods (*vṛddhaśravāḥ*) in the Vedic literature. Here Indra is Vedic, not Purāṇic. Indra represents the life-force aspect of the universal Cosmic Power. The same Cosmic Power reflects in the body-mind complex of an individual. Normally, a person is endowed with five organs of action and five sense-organs. All the ten organs function under the supervision of the mind, which is considered as the inner organ. These eleven organs are called *indriya*s, because they function by the grace of Lord Indra.

इन्द्रेण परमेश्वरेण दत्तं इन्द्रेण जुष्टं इति इन्द्रियम् ।

indreṇa parameśvareṇa dattaṁ indreṇa juṣṭaṁ iti indriyam ।

> The organs of action and the sense-organs are called *indriya*s because they are bestowed upon the individual by Indra, the Lord, and they also function by the grace of Indra.

We invoke the blessings of Indra who represents the forces of strength and vitality at the universal as well as at the individual level. Thus, the prayer connects the individual with the whole and there is liberation from the bondage of *saṁsāra* in such a cognitive connection.

Svasti naḥ pūṣā viśvavedāḥ. The Sun god is called Pūṣan (*puṣṇāti iti pūṣan*), since the Sun sustains life on the earth. The Purāṇic Viṣṇu, the sustainer of the universe, and the Vedic Sun are the same. The Sun, who illuminates the entire planetary system, also stands for spiritual knowledge. Lord Śrī Kṛṣṇa says in the *Gītā* that the Sun was the very first student of Self-knowledge. In knowing the Self, everything else is effectively known. Hence, the Sun god is Omniscient (*viśvavedāḥ*). It is also said that Hanumān, known to be very intelligent, was a student of the Sun god. The sage

Yājñavalkya, the seer of the *Śukla Yajurveda*, was also a student of the Sun god. Besides the vitality of a functional existence, a human being also needs knowledge and intelligence. Therefore, we seek the most auspicious in the form of the liberating knowledge of the Self from the Sun god.

Svasti nastārkṣyo ariṣṭanemiḥ. Tārkṣya means the divine eagle Garuḍa, the chief of birds, who serves as a vehicle for Lord Viṣṇu. He is one of the important gods in the Vedic literature. He is also described in the *Taittirīya Upaniṣad* as *suparṇa,* one with graceful feathers. In that Upaniṣad (2-5), *Brahman*, the ultimate Reality, is metaphorically presented as the tail of a bird (*brahma puccham pratiṣṭhā*), since *Brahman* bestows existence and sustenance to this world of names and forms, like the tail provides stability to the bird in flight. The god Garuḍa, the offspring of the omniscient sage Tarkṣa or Kaśyapa, is known to dispel evil forces and inauspicious things from the lives of the devotees. There is always a possibility of a few undesirable things happening in life. Sometimes, people we love may not be doing well for a variety of reasons. Here we pray that such *ariṣṭa*s (misfortunes) are not visited upon us; if inevitable, their power to hurt us may be mitigated. Further, may our capacity to withstand such calamities grow. In the *Taittirīya Saṁhitā,* the Lord worshipped in the altar of fire is eulogized as the chief of birds, Garutmān. Since the Lord is Omniscient, various aspects of Vedic knowledge are metaphorically presented as different limbs of Garutmān.

Svasti no bṛhaspatirdadhātu. Bṛhaspati, the *guru* of gods, is same as Jupiter, the most important of all the planets. Even from the point of view of size, it is the largest planet, and after the Sun, it exerts the maximum gravitational force. If Bṛhaspati is propitiated and worshipped, it amounts to worshipping and propitiating all the other planets as well.

Oṁ śāntiḥ śāntiḥ śāntiḥ. Śānti means peace of mind. Generally people think that what they seek in life are certain objects and the company of loved ones. But, what people really need and seek through all of the objects and other people is peace of mind alone. Instead of blindly running after pleasures, we should accord a premium value to peace of mind in our life. Here, *śānti* repeated thrice refers to the cessation of the three-fold afflictions in life. They are: *ādhyātmika* — problems related to the physical body as in ill-health; *ādhibhautika* — problems caused by harmful persons like thieves; and *ādhidaivika* — problems like excess or scant rain caused by the gods.

After the invocatory prayer, the Upaniṣad proper starts as:

ओं नमस्ते गणपतये ।। १ ।।

oṁ namaste gaṇapataye ॥ 1 ॥

My prostration unto the Lord Gaṇapati.

Gaṇapataye namaḥ. The word *namaḥ* has a very interesting etymology. Literally it means bowing the head with devotion in front of an altar of the Lord. It indicates humility on the part of the devotee. Etymologically, *na me* is *namaḥ*, which means "not mine." In this creation, nothing really belongs to us — not even the physical body. Everything belongs to the Lord. We come utterly alone into this world and leave it the same way. But, due to ignorance we assume that we own a few things; sometimes, even a few persons. This sense of ownership is rooted in ignorance. While uttering *namaḥ* before the Lord, we strive to neutralize this wrong notion of ownership. That is the real meaning of *namaḥ* and a true devotee is supposed to utter it with such a feeling. The sense of "me" and "mine" is very deeply ingrained in our psyche. Therefore, it is imperative to repeatedly disown the false connection with the things of the world. So, we utter the word *namaḥ* again and again.

The Lord alone has manifested as the five great elements, namely, space, wind, fire, waters and earth. They are the fundamental building blocks of this universe. For example, let us look at a rock and a tree. One is a living form and the other is inanimate. Despite this obvious difference between the two, both have evolved essentially from the same five elements. With a particular configuration of these elements, a rock is formed. The same five elements, when combined in a different configuration, have the ability to form an organism that reflects life. This also applies to a human being. The human body that you consider to be you or yours is just another configuration of the five elements. These five elements are given to us; they do not belong to anyone, nor are they created by anyone. It is this understanding that is reflected in the utterance *namaḥ*.

The Lord's name is Gaṇapati here. Let us understand the word Gaṇapati. We can look at this word from two different angles — the theological and the etymological. It is clearly understood in the Hindu philosophy that the Lord, the ultimate Reality, has no specific form (*nirguṇa nirākāra*), and hence the devotee can worship Him in any form of his choice, called Personal God (*saguṇa sākāra* or *īṣṭa daiva*). Every such form of the Personal God is associated with a story, often from the Purāṇas.

Generally, one takes oneself to be a limited individual isolated from the Whole. But, every individual is an indivisible part of the Whole. In the *Gītā* (15.7) Lord Śrī Kṛṣṇa describes the individual as follows:

ममैवांशो जीवलोके जीवभूतस्सनातनः ।

mamaivāṁśo jīvaloke jīvabhūtassanātanaḥ ।

This individual in the world of individuals is indeed eternal and is a part of Me alone.

As the individual fails to recognize this truth and isolates himself from the Whole, he suffers. As the individual grows in the knowledge of his unity with the Whole, he is liberated from the travails of life. Devotion unto and the worship of the Lord facilitates in establishing this connectedness between the individual and the Whole. It is generally believed that the worship of the Lord by the individual in a form chosen and liked by him is easier than worshipping God as the formless Reality. The worship of the Personal God becomes relevant in an individual's devotional life from this point of view. As long as one takes oneself to be a limited individual, one should understand that one is never separated from the Whole. One has to connect oneself with the Whole by constant worship, *upāsanā*, of the Personal God. The Hindu worship is truly democratic in spirit. One can choose the form of the Lord suitable to one's own disposition from among the forms presented by the Vedic sages. One of the most important and popular of these forms is Gaṇapati.

The Lord is called Śiva, the Auspicious, since for the devotee, the Lord alone is auspicious and sacred. The creative faculty or the infinite Power of the Lord is Śakti, also called Pārvatī in the Purāṇas. Gaṇapati is the offspring of Śiva and Śakti, a combination of the attributeless *Brahman* and the Power that is the origin of the universe. Thus, Gaṇapati is the *saguṇa* (with attributes) *Brahman*.

Etymologically, Gaṇapati means the Lord of the groups. In this creation, all living beings exist and thrive in groups, each of these groups being a *gaṇa*. This psychology of living in groups equally applies to the gods, the humans and other life forms. All these groups exist in one Supreme Reality, the *Brahman*. That is why It is called Gaṇapati — the Supreme Lord of the *gaṇa*s. The same idea is expressed in the popular *mantra* of the *Taittirīya Saṁhitā* (2-3-14) as follows:

गणानां त्वा गणपतिं हवामहे कविं कवीनामुपमश्रवस्तमम् ।

ज्येष्ठराजं ब्रह्मणां ब्रह्मणस्पत आ नश्शृण्वन्नूतिभिस्सीद सादनम् ।।

gaṇānāṁ tvā gaṇapatiṁ havāmahe kaviṁ kavīnāmupama-śravastamam ।
jyeṣṭharājaṁ brahmaṇāṁ brahmaṇaspata ānaśśṛṇvan-nūtibhissīda sādanam ।।

O Lord of all *mantra*s, we invite you, the Supreme Lord of all the groups in the universe. You are the supreme among the learned and your fame has no parallel even among the famous. You are the King of the kings. Please take your seat in this ritual, listen to the encomiums sung by us, and bestow upon us all kinds of wealth.

The gods exist in groups. For example, the Vasus constitute a group of eight, Rudras of eleven, Ādityas of twelve, and Aśvinīs of two. Maruts are a group of seven sub-groups, each sub-group again having seven members, totalling forty-nine members in all. The sunlight is a composition of seven colours. The galaxies exist in clusters. The planets constitute a system. At the micro-level, atoms come together to form molecules, which in turn have a tertiary structure of their own assemblies. There are no independent entities in this creation; there are only systems.

It is well known that man is a social animal. People come together in all kinds of groupings based on caste, creed, religion, race, geographic origin, etc. In any society, one finds all kinds of associations, like Association of Businessmen, of Agriculturists, of Scientists, of government

workers, of the handicapped, of the blind, of the consumers,
of the train travellers and so on. Abused women have an
association. Believe me, henpecked husbands too have an
association! Cine-goers have an association of their own.
All the nations of the world have formed a group called
the United Nations. Organized religion is an expression of
this psychology of grouping among humans. Even agnostics
and atheists have their own associations. Beggars too have
their associations.

"No man is an island," they say, and I substitute man
with *jīva*. Every individual is a part of the Whole; that apart,
even in a limited sense, the individual is part of a group. In
modern societies, the ideas of individuality and personal
freedom are overemphasized. This is wrong. The more one
stresses personal freedom and individuality, the more
miserable one becomes. One could easily extend this logic
of personal freedom to justify one's craving for sensual
pleasures. People want freedom in full measure, because
they want to enjoy life in full measure. This is a misplaced
connection between personal freedom and sense pleasures.
One can have real happiness only when one dilutes one's
sense of personality and individuality by gradually
surrendering them at the altar of the Whole.

If in a family of four, each has his or her own room and
eats his or her own food at the time of his or her own
convenience and each manages his or her own finances,
and meets others only while leaving and entering their
rooms through a common hall, it does not make for a
desirable lifestyle. The desirable lifestyle would be the one
that brings all the family members together at an appointed
time, to pray together in addition to their individual prayers,
and to eat together. That gives each one of them an identity
as a member of the family. Such an identity should be
nurtured. Otherwise, the young tend to develop an identity

in which the family bond becomes very weak. They won't hesitate to break up with the family, if it does not suit them. As long as the association with the family is convenient for them, they go along. But at the first instance of friction, they break up with the family. They argue that the individual freedom is the only thing that matters. This is a sociological phenomenon.

Every individual is part of a group. He should not remain in an island. He should relate to the bigger picture. The bigger the group, the happier the person. I came across an article titled "An anthropology of happiness" in the magazine The Economist (22 December 2001), based on a survey conducted by a University Professor. A community of immigrant workers from a poor country working in a prosperous city was studied. Those workers don't have a place to live. Sometimes they sleep in the kitchens where they work. Some of them sleep in a corner of the garage or gas station where they are employed. Some even sleep in a corner cupboard lying vacant. They carry on with this kind of "bare minimum" lifestyle, and all the money they earn is sent home. Their families back home live comfortably. They work everyday of the week and congregate once a week at some place to socialize with fellow workers and to have some nice time; they eat together and then disperse.

Then there are their employers. They strictly maintain their individuality and personal freedom, which they consider very important in life. The workers have no personal freedom and have no place to call their own and most of the money that they earn is sent home. They are merely part of a huge machinery. Their lifestyle is described as "shared being." Despite such contrasting lifestyles, the study revealed that the employers as a group were significantly less happy than the workers. The secret of the workers' happiness is their identification with a group and the resultant reduction of the emphasis on personal fulfilment. In their mind, the sense of "belonging" (being part of the whole) is much stronger than that of their individuality. That proved to be the source of their happiness. We should never isolate ourselves from the group, family or community. This truth is instinctively recognized by every life form, except humans in some instances. It appears that this grouping psychology applies to the gods also.

The lower forms of life exhibit a strong sense of group psychology. Have you ever noticed the birds flying in a V-formation? It is not the individual bird that flies forward; it is the V that moves forward. If a bird suddenly strays out of the formation, all the other birds, as it were, frown upon it; they instinctively encourage and help it to return to the formation. For the V to move forward, the velocity has to be perfectly maintained by each bird. Animals are, of course, known to move in herds. Birds, animals, fish, etc., live in groups and migrate in groups. The group behaviour among monkeys, elephants, ants, bees, etc., is well documented in scientific literature. I happened to observe ants prowling around for food particles, and when they do so, it is not that each ant is on its own for its own food; it is the group working for the benefit of the entire group. Even if one ant strays, it will soon come back into the group. Even bacteria never occur as individuals, but appear always in clusters. It is obvious that flora exist as forests. All these groups exist in one Supreme Reality called *Brahman*. Gaṇapati is the Supreme Lord of all these innumerable groups, bestowing existence and sustenance upon them.

The word *Gaṇapati* has a cosmological connotation too. In Vedic Cosmology, there is no special creation; there is only manifestation. *Māyā śakti* is the manifesting Power of the Lord; it is also called *avyakta*, the Unmanifest. It manifests as the *mahat*, the Universal Intelligence, which further manifests as the *ahaṅkāra*, the Universal Ego. The latter manifests as the five subtle elements, which in turn manifest as the gross elements. All these primary principles, starting from the Unmanifest up to the gross elements, constitute a group. This group of basic building blocks of the universe has originated from the Lord and exists in the Lord. Hence, the Lord is appropriately called Gaṇapati.

त्वमेव प्रत्यक्षं तत्त्वमसि ।

tvameva pratyakṣaṁ tattvamasi ।

You alone are the Reality manifest before us (as the universe).

Tattvam means reality. What appears real to the senses and the mind may not be real. In fact, we define reality as "an existence that is not affected or influenced by time." In other words, it cannot be negated in any of the three periods of time — past, present or future (*trikālābādhitam satyam*). For instance, consider a pot. We don't call the pot real, because it did not exist before a particular time, and also it will not be there after a while. Even an antique pot will some day cease to exist. The reality of a pot is clay. Clay alone, obtaining in a particular spatial configuration for a length of time, is viewed as a pot. Therefore, a pot is nothing but a name corresponding to a form; it is unreal (*mithyā*). With reference to the pot, clay alone is real.

Tattvam is also defined as *anāropitākāram*; it means Reality that is not limited by a form which is but a superimposition. This universe is nothing but so many names and forms superimposed on the underlying Reality of Existence Absolute that is *Brahman*. That *Brahman* is worshipped here as Gaṇapati. Though *Brahman* as the

Reality is beyond the scope of sense-organs (perception)
and mind (inference, etc.), its glory manifests before us in
the form of universe. Whatever direction we may look at,
that direction is ablaze with Divinity. In this context, we
may remember the glorious *mantra* of the *Muṇḍakopaniṣad*
(2-2-11):

ब्रह्मैवेदममृतं पुरस्ताद्ब्रह्म पश्चाद्ब्रह्म दक्षिणतश्चोत्तरेण ।

अधश्चोर्ध्वं च प्रसृतं ब्रह्मैवेदं विश्वमिदं वरिष्ठम् ।।

brahmaivedamamṛtaṁ purastādbrahma paścādbrahma
dakṣiṇataścottareṇa ।

adhaścordhvaṁ ca prasṛtaṁ brahmaivedaṁ viśvamidaṁ
variṣṭham ।।

Whatever is in the front is this Immortal *Brahman*
alone. *Brahman* alone is at the back. *Brahman* alone
is on the right and *Brahman* alone is on the left.
Brahman alone pervades above and below. This
universe is indeed the almighty *Brahman*.

When we view the world of names and forms as real, there
is plenty of scope for fostering likes and dislikes. The
moment we visualize or understand that the underlying
Reality of this world is *Brahman*, the likes and dislikes
disappear that very moment. For example, when we look
at a shirt, the question of liking or disliking it arises, but
with reference to the fabric of the shirt liking and disliking
have no relevance. That is the reason why Vedānta attempts
to turn the attention of the person away from the *saṁsāra*
of names and forms to the underlying Reality. This immortal
message of the Upaniṣads is echoed in the very first verse
of the *Īśāvāsyopaniṣad* :

ईशावास्यमिदं सर्वं यत्किञ्च जगत्यां जगत् ।

īśāvāsyamidaṁ sarvaṁ yatkiṁ ca jagatyāṁ jagat ।

Whatever exists in this creation, all that has to be covered (understood as pervaded) by the Lord.

We have analysed *pratyakṣaṁ tattvam* with reference to *adhibhūta*, the outside world. Now, we will analyse it with reference to *adhyātma*, the body-mind-sense complex. The word *pratyakṣaṁ* (*prati-akṣaṁ*) means "with reference to every sense-organ." *Brahman* (the Supreme Reality) alone manifests as eye-sight through the pair of eyes; It manifests as the hearing through ears and so on. It is the reflection of the Universal Power in the body that makes this body alive. The individual's claim that they are "my" eyes, "my" ears, "my" heart, etc., is rooted in ignorance. Every faculty in every life form is a glorious manifestation of *Brahman*. The objects of thoughts may vary widely, but the essential content of each and every thought is the same Awareness which is *ātman* that is *Brahman*. Even the background reality of the I-thought, which is an individual, is indeed *Brahman*. This vision is presented beautifully in the following verse of the *Kenopaniṣad* (1-2) :

श्रोत्रस्य श्रोत्रं मनसो मनो यद्वाचो ह वाचं स उ प्राणस्य प्राण: ।
चक्षुषश्चक्षुरतिमुच्य धीरा: प्रेत्यास्माल्लोकादमृता भवन्ति ।।

śrotrasya śrotraṁ manaso mano yadvāco ha vācaṁ sa u prāṇasya prāṇaḥ ।
cakṣuṣaścakṣuratimucya dhīrāḥ pretyāsmāllokādamṛtā bhavanti ।।

It is the ear of the ear and the mind of the mind; It is the speech of the speech and the *prāṇa* (the vital breath) of the *prāṇa*. Knowing It as the eye of the eye, the wise rising above the identification with the body and the senses gain Immortality.

It is the One non-dual Supreme Reality that is expressing through every sense-organ of every life form in this creation. The ears, eyes, etc., are the equipments (*upādhi*s) that express *Brahman*. This is the meaning of the expression *pratyakṣaṁ tattvam*. If the world represents the ornaments, *Brahman* represents gold. The difference between any two ornaments is unreal, as the difference is only in name and form, while gold, the commonality between them, is real. Similarly, Awareness is common to all pulses of knowledge in a person. It is also common to all conscious beings. If the world represents waves, then *Brahman* represents water. If the world represents the scenes on a movie screen, then *Brahman* represents the lighted screen.

त्वमेव केवलं कर्ताऽसि । त्वमेव केवलं धर्ताऽसि । त्वमेव केवलं हर्ताऽसि ।

tvameva kevalaṁ kartā'si ı tvameva kevalaṁ dhartā'si ı tvameva kevalaṁ hartā'si ı

You alone are the creator; you alone are the sustainer; you alone are the annihilator.

There are countless phenomena that occur each moment in every nook and corner of this vast universe. But at the macro-level, the scriptures always talk of the three most important phenomena, viz., the creation, sustenance and annihilation of this universe. Any description of the Lord focuses on these three universal phenomena. In fact, the Upaniṣadic definition of the Lord is based on these three universal phenomena as shown in the famous *Brahmasūtra* (1-1-2) :

जन्माद्यस्य यतः ।

janmādyasya yataḥ ı

Brahman is that from which this universe originates, in which it is sustained, and into which it resolves.

There is a widespread notion that three different gods perform the functions of creation, sustenance and annihilation. This belief is based on the lack of proper understanding of the scriptures. Consider the following verse from the *Śrīmadbhāgavatam* (4-7-51):

आत्ममायां समाविश्य सोऽहं गुणमयीं द्विज ।

सृजन् रक्षन् हरन् विश्वं दधे संज्ञां क्रियोचिताम् ।।

ātmamāyāṁ samāviśya so'haṁ guṇamayīṁ dvija ǀ sṛjan rakṣan haran viśvaṁ dadhre sañjñāṁ kriyocitām ǀǀ

O Vidura, Reflecting in my *māyā* (the Universal Power) composed of the three *guṇas, sattva, rajas,* and *tamas*, I create this universe, I sustain it and I annihilate it. I assume three different names in accordance with the acts I perform.

There are any number of such statements not only in the *Śrīmadbhāgavatam*, but also in every other scripture. That Lord may be called Viṣṇu or Śiva, but He is called Gaṇapati in this Upaniṣad. The difference is only verbal or nominal.

त्वमेव सर्वं खल्विदं ब्रह्मासि । त्वं साक्षादात्माऽसि नित्यम् ।। २ ।।

tvameva sarvaṁ khalvidaṁ brahmāsi ǀ tvaṁ sākṣādātmā'si nityam ǀǀ 2 ǀǀ

All this is *Brahman* and you are that *Brahman*. You are indeed the *ātman* all the time.

The Supreme Reality, which is the substratum of this entire creation, is called *Brahman* (*niratiśayaṁ bṛhat*, infinitely large). Being the origin of both space and time together with the entire world of names and forms, It is beyond the limitations of space and time. The universe appears manifold, and we take it as real. But it is not so. In the background of space and time framework alone, the Existence Absolute appears as many. The non-dual *Brahman* alone is the Reality of this manifold appearance called the world. This profound spiritual vision finds expression here as well as in the other terse Śruti statement *sarvaṁ khalvidaṁ brahma* meaning all that is here is *Brahman*.

It is easy to understand that this entire universe with all its variety and diversity is nothing but permutations and combinations of the five great elements: the earth, the waters, fire, wind and space. Some of these combinations are organic in nature and they reflect Life, which is the power of the Lord, whereas the inorganic ones do not. Thus the universe is reduced to five basic elements as a first step towards the realization of the Supreme Reality. These five elements, in their turn, are the same Existence Absolute, merely with a different name and form. Thus, the earth is the grossest manifestation of the Existence, while space is the subtlest. The other three elements occupy the intermediate positions. Therefore, the same Existence is "tapered" to give rise to the appearance of the five great elements. Thus in the vision of the enlightened sages the entire universe is reduced to the non-dual Existence Absolute, the *Brahman*. This vision is termed as *sad-vidyā*.

Having resolved the universe into the Lord, we have to do the same thing with the individual so as to complete the marvellous journey to the ultimate Reality. Just as there is a world outside me, there is a world within me. First, there is this body which has its existence in the sense-organs, because without them there is no body. The body is perceived as a result of integration of all the sensations caused by the five sense-organs. These sense-organs, in turn, have their existence in the mind. The mind, in turn, exists in the ego; and the ego exists in Awareness that is the *ātman*.

All the limitations of the ego are superimposed on the limitless Awareness. For instance, we know how subtle an atom is. But the mind, through which we know it, has to be subtler than the atom, because in knowing, the atom becomes an object of the mind. This is quite like saying that the mind that made the computer possible is superior to the computer. The ego is superior to this mind, because it is the ego that wields the mind as an instrument for knowing the things of the world. The ego, in turn, is like a whirlpool in the limitless Awareness. So, in a way, the ego is the child of the Awareness, and the pity is that the child overshadows its parent — the source. When one understands this truth, the ego weakens. As it weakens, the underlying Awareness (*cit*) comes into focus. Finally, when the ego is resolved, there is only the Infinite *ātman* which is *Brahman*. Because the ego identifies itself with the physical body, it is subject to the limitations of time and space. In the *ātman* the limitations of time and space do not exist. This vision may be termed as *cid-vidyā*.

The final Truth can be arrived at through either the *sat*-aspect or the *cit*-aspect of the *Brahman*. Here the word *sākṣāt* is very significant. Let us examine it further. There are a few categories of the things that are known to the knower, the individual. Things like a pot, etc., that are perceived by the knower through the sense-organs are called *pratyakṣa*. Those like heaven which are not available for direct perception are called *parokṣa*. The moods of the mind, like pleasure or pain, are neither *pratyakṣa* like a pot, nor *parokṣa* like heaven. They form a distinct category called *aparokṣa*. That leaves the essential content of the knower himself, the self-evident Awareness that is *ātman*, which is the eternal witness of all the above categories. It is called *sākṣī* or *sākṣāt aparokṣa*, and it is *Brahman*.

ऋतं वच्मि । सत्यं वच्मि ॥ ३ ॥

ṛtaṁ vacmi, satyaṁ vacmi ॥ 3 ॥

I declare (that You are the) *ṛtaṁ*. I declare (that You are the) *satyaṁ*.

Both ṛta and satya mean the same, the truth. But there is an important difference in their meanings when both the words are used together. Ṛta is the knowledge fully ascertained by the study of scriptures, whereas satya is the same knowledge expressed in speech and action. The life in this body is entirely dependent upon the Whole which is the Lord. Hence, all the functions of the body depend on the all-pervading Lord. So, we can identify any given function with the Lord. The faculties of thinking, speech and acting are the expressions of the Universal Power of the Lord in the devotee's equipments, the body and the mind. Hence, the devotee uses his sāttvika will to declare this understanding or knowledge, and its expression through speech and action is the manifestation of the Divinity within the person. This understanding opens the door to the Supreme Truth which is Brahman.

These two words ṛta and satya can also be understood in another way. There are two orders of reality in this creation — the empirical and the absolute. In the example of the pot and clay, the pot is nothing but a name and a form. Hence, the pot belongs to the order of empirical reality, while the clay belongs to the order of absolute reality. Similarly, it may be understood that this entire creation is empirically real, whereas the substratum of the creation, the Brahman, is the Absolute Reality. But, we should be alert to the fact that there is only One non-dual Brahman and the world is a superimposition on It. The appearance cannot exist outside or without the Real. Therefore, the same non-dual Brahman despite appearing as the world remains eternal in Its own supreme glory. Ṛta is the empirical reality, while satya is the Absolute Reality. The devotee declares that both are the Brahman.

Further, ṛta is the order that holds the universe together as the cosmos. In the absence of this universal order, there would be only chaos. For example, this *ṛta* expresses as the gravitational field that sustains the orbital motion of the planets around the Sun. *Satya* is the Absolute Reality, the substratum of this universal order. In this *mantra*, the devotee recognizes that both *ṛta* and *satya* are Gaṇapati alone.

Or, the devotee is simply declaring his intention to speak truth and nothing but the truth. But we should note that it is not enough to speak the truth (*satya*) as one knows it. We should ascertain its veracity (*ṛta*) before conveying it to others. It is not uncommon that people who mean well end up misleading others, because they themselves do not bother to fully ascertain what they convey.

अव त्वं माम् । अव वक्तारम् । अव श्रोतारम् । अव दातारम् ।
अव धातारम् । अवानूचानमव शिष्यम् ।।

*ava tvaṁ mām ı ava vaktāram ı ava śrotāram ı
ava dātāram ı ava dhātāram ı avānūcānamava
śiṣyam ıı*

Protect me. Protect the teacher of this Upaniṣad. Protect the one who listens to this Upaniṣad. Protect the one who initiates the devotees into your worship. Protect the one who commits this Upaniṣad to memory. Protect the student who recites this Upaniṣad after the teacher. Protect the student who studies the meaning of this Upaniṣad.

This is the prayer of the teacher on his own behalf and on behalf of his disciples. In the ancient tradition of Vedic teaching, every teacher is a student, and every student will eventually be a teacher. Knowledge can be safeguarded only by protecting the teachers and students of that knowledge. It is our common experience that a sincere seeker of knowledge is always plagued by all kinds of obstacles. Hence the prayer to ward off all such obstacles in the path of knowledge is indeed in the fitness of things. Initiating the deserving person into this worship and knowledge is considered a very pious act. Hence, the prayer of this *mantra* is for the protection of such wise people who initiate the seekers.

The primary means for developing devotion to the Lord and gaining Self-knowledge is listening to the exposition of the scriptures by the teacher (*śravaṇam*). Hence, the seeker who listens to the exposition of this Upaniṣad is included in the prayer. Daily recitation of this Upaniṣad is an integral part of the worship of the Lord. Hence, the prayer recommends that the student may commit the Upaniṣad to memory.

This knowledge can be gained by the seeker only from a teacher belonging to the teaching tradition of *brahmavidyā*. It is a mandate to the student to recite after the teacher, pronouncing the *mantra*s exactly the way the teacher pronounces them. This is the only way to ensure correct intonations in reciting the *mantra*s. The intonations are very important because any change in them can bring in an altogether different or opposite meaning. Finally, the student is expected to know the meaning of the *mantra*s, once he masters the chanting.

अव पुरस्तात्तात् । अव दक्षिणात्तात् । अव पश्चात्तात् ।
अवोत्तरात्तात् । अव चोर्ध्वात्तात् । अवाधरात्तात् । सर्वतो मां
पाहि पाहि समन्तात् ॥ ४ ॥

*ava purastāttāt ı ava dakṣiṇāttāt ı ava paścāttāt ı
avottarāttāt ı ava cordhvāttāt ı avādharāttāt ı
sarvato māṁ pāhi pāhi samantāt ıı 4 ıı*

> Protect me from whatever (adversity) that is attracted from the east, south, west, north, from above and below. Protect me without fail (from the obstacles that may arise) from all directions and in all possible ways.

The earlier verse was all about the teacher, student and the knowledge. Now comes a more general prayer. Here Gaṇapati is addressed as the Cosmic Person who manifests as this physical world. An obstacle or a danger can be visited upon us from any direction. Hence, we seek protection in all directions. The word *ātta* (acquired or attracted) is significant. It occurs in all these sentences except the last. Thus, the meaning is — "Protect me from whatever (adversity) that I might have attracted from the south, the west, the north, and from above and below." Any adversity that may be visited upon the human being is indeed brought in by him alone. The role of the Lord is only to grant the results of actions to the individuals. Recognizing this universal law, the devotee seeks to neutralize, at least partially, the ill effects of the future events with the grace of the Lord earned through this prayer.

As we transact our affairs in the world, we acquire a lot of things and develop relationships, both good and bad. These bind us to the world and make our outlook extrovert and worldly; thereby we become psychologically dependent on the things and the people of the world. Sometimes the mere rememberance of these acquisitions is enough to make us unhappy. This is how *saṁsāra* envelopes us. We have to develop non-identification and non-attachment with respect to them. This is easier said than done. Hence, we need all the grace of the Lord for gaining this wisdom. We find in these *mantras* a lot of repetition of words like *ava*. This is the general style of Vedic prayers.

That which is accumulated from "above" and from "below" refer to the *puṇya* (merit) and the *pāpa* (sin) respectively. Wrong doing takes the individual (*jīva*) to hell, and good deeds to heaven. For a devotee who seeks liberation, even heaven is considered a bondage. Thus, the devotee earnestly seeks protection of the Lord from everything and from all directions.

त्वं वाङ्मयस्त्वं चिन्मयः । त्वमानन्दमयस्त्वं ब्रह्ममयः ।।

tvaṁ vāṅmayastvaṁ cinmayaḥ ı tvamānanda-
mayastvaṁ brahmamayaḥ ıı

You are in the form of the sounds (words). You are in the form of consciousness. You are in the form of Happiness. You are the *Brahman*, the Existence Absolute, the source of all existence in this creation.

The universe is nothing but a conglomeration of countless forms with corresponding names. Each form is associated with a name. There is no intrinsic reality for the form. Hence, all forms are reduced to corresponding names, which in turn, have their origin in the Lord. Thus, the Lord who is the origin of this universe of forms is obviously the origin of all names too. Further, this universe of names and forms comes to light only in the consciousness, since names and forms do not shine by themselves. That consciousness is also the manifestation of the same Lord. In fact, forms are the manifestation of the *sat*-aspect of the Lord; the consciousness in which these forms come to light is the manifestation of the *cit*-aspect of the Lord. Names which are the bridge between the forms and one's consciousness are also the manifestation of the Lord.

The Lord, the *ātman* (the essential content) of all living beings, is not limited in time, space or as an object. Hence the Lord is called Infinite. The dynamic expression of the Infinitude of the *ātman* is *ānanda*, happiness. There is no happiness in this creation other than that of *ātman*. The objects of the world do not possess happiness. Due to ignorance, we assume that the objects give us happiness. Happiness is indeed the essential nature of *ātman*.

Ananta and *ānanda* have to be correlated. A limitation is an imperfection and hence the cause of all sorrow. The limitation or imperfection, when addressed and eliminated, leads to the sense of completeness, which is happiness. The human being identifies with the imperfect ego which constantly projects its imperfection in the form of various desires. In the event of a desire getting fulfilled, the imperfection disappears for a short while, and the ego resolves in its source, the *ātman*. The person experiences happiness till the ego projects yet another desire. One mistakenly thinks that the gratified desire has given happiness. In reality, the happiness has its origin in *ātman*. Happiness is not a property of the external things. The external things may help in the communion with the inner Self, which is the inexhaustible source of happiness. Life itself exists because of this happiness; it is sustained by an occasional tapping of the happiness from that inner source. This glory of *ātman* is beautifully highlighted in the following *mantra* of the *Bṛhadāraṇyakopaniṣad* (4-3-32) :

एषोऽस्य परम आनन्द एतस्यैवानन्दस्यान्यानि भूतानि मात्रामुपजीवन्ति ।

eṣo'sya parama ānanda etasyaivānandasyānyāni bhūtāni mātrāmupajīvanti ।

This is the eternal Happiness (*ānanda*) of the person. The other life forms (apparently separated from the *ātman* by ignorance) sustain their life by abiding in a speck of this Happiness (*ānanda*).

Whatever happiness a person may get is tapped from this one source of happiness, the *ātman* which is *Brahman*. All life forms receive their share of happiness commensurate with their merits from this one source.

तवं सच्चिदानन्दाऽद्वितीयोऽसि । तवं प्रत्यक्षं ब्रह्मासि ।।

tvaṁ saccidānandā'dvitīyo'si ι tvaṁ pratyakṣaṁ brahmāsi ιι

You are the non-dual Existence-Awareness-Happiness Absolute. You are *Brahman* manifest before us.

We have seen that *Brahman* is the Existence Absolute (*sat*), the Infinite Awareness (*cit*) and the Happiness Absolute (*ānanda*). Are these three different attributes of *Brahman*? No. What "is", that alone "shines." What "shines," that alone "is." The difference between what is (*asti*) and what shines (*bhāti*) is purely verbal, like the difference between the dream and the dreamer. Human beings, accustomed to the identification with the physical body, place the "being" on the "outside," and the knowing-ness in the "inside," as they take the body line as the boundary between inside and outside, entirely due to the ignorance of the nature of the all-pervading *Brahman*. Either everything is "inside" with reference to *ātman*, since everything shines in Awareness that is *ātman*; or everything is "outside," since *ātman* is distinct from everything that is unreal. Thus, being and knowing-ness are one and the same. This *sat-cit* is beyond all limitations, and so is Happiness. Thus, *Brahman* is the non-dual Reality, which alone appears as existence, consciousness and happiness. That *Brahman* is addressed as Gaṇapati in this Upaniṣad.

तवं प्रत्यक्षं ब्रह्मासि । तवं ज्ञानमयो विज्ञानमयोऽसि ।। ५ ।।

*tvaṁ pratyakṣaṁ brahmāsi ι tvaṁ jñānamayo
vijñānamayo'si* ιι 5 ιι

You are the *Brahman* present before us in the
form of the world. You alone are in the form
of the awareness and the consciousness.

There is a general impression that it is very difficult to attain
Godhead (that is liberation). But, here the Upaniṣad holds
the contrary viewpoint. *Brahman* abides in the heart of every
living being all the time as the innermost core. There is no
need to search for Him, as if He has hidden somewhere. It
is just enough to negate the name and form and reject
identification with body and intellect as well as other
psychological and cultural conditioning to accomplish
immediate oneness with the Lord.

God is omnipresent. One may think that God is a person,
finite and other than oneself. This is not the way to realize
the Truth. The true realization is to see God everywhere
and in everything. The entire creation is to be cognitively
enveloped in Divinity. The *Mahānārāyaṇopaniṣad* (13)
declares as follows:

अन्तर्बहिश्च तत्सर्वं व्याप्य नारायणस्थितः ।।

antarbahiśca tatsarvaṁ vyāpya nārāyaṇassthitaḥ ιι

Lord Nārāyaṇa pervades everything in the creation
both within and without.

One very significant manifestation of *Bramhan* is as the life-
giving *vāyu* (air). Every time we inhale and exhale, we
establish communion with the Whole. During inhalation,
the entire organism gets rejuvenated, and during exhalation
all toxins produced in the body are eliminated. Hence, air
is described very appropriately in the *Taittirīyopaniṣad* (1-
1) as the *pratyakṣaṁ brahma*, the *Brahman* directly
experienced.

नमस्ते वायो । त्वमेव प्रत्यक्षं ब्रह्मासि ।।

namaste vāyo ı tvameva pratyakṣaṁ brahmāsi ıı

O Vāyu, my prostration unto you. You are the *Brahman* directly perceived (through the sense of touch).

Both the words *jñāna* and *vijñāna* mean knowledge. But, there is a significant difference in the meaning of these words when they are used together. In the *Gītā* we find such a differentiation quite often. In fact, in the *Gītā*, we have a chapter called *jñāna-vijñāna yoga*. Indirect knowledge of *Brahman* gained by the seeker by listening to the scriptures is called *jñāna*. This knowledge is indirect as the seeker may still have a few doubts about it; his orientation may still be opposed to this knowledge. Such a seeker must reflect upon the teaching and contemplate upon his own nature in accordance with the teaching. It is only the relentless reflection and contemplation that eventually enables the seeker to assimilate the knowledge revealed by the scriptures. Only then, it is termed direct knowledge, *vijñāna*. Both these types of knowledge are indeed the culmination of the grace of the Lord.

In the ritual section of the Vedas, *jñāna* means the theoretical knowledge, for example, the knowledge of the knowhow of a ritual. This knowledge is incomplete unless put in practice. The will and the skill deployed in putting such a knowledge into practice in performing the ritual is called *vijñāna*. It may be stated again that these two types of knowledge are the direct result of the grace of the Lord.

Jñāna is the knowledge by which the seeker recognizes the One cause behind the multiple effects. On the other hand, appreciation of the process by which the One cause becomes many effects is called *vijñāna*. Recognition of the attributeless *Brahman* as the Existence-Absolute substratum of this plurality of the creation is *jñāna*, while the appreciation of the manifestation of the non-dual *Brahman* with the limiting adjunct of the *māyā-śakti* as the manifold universe is *vijñāna*. Again, both are gained due to the grace of the Lord.

"I am" is the *ātman*, as it is the most fundamental movement in the Awareness that is *ātman*. This "I am" is homogeneous and undifferentiated and hence attributeless. Such a knowledge is called *jñāna*. This "I am" alone manifests in every pulsation of knowledge in the mind. The knowledge of forms, sounds, smell, touch and taste takes place in the mind, which is nothing but a movement on the substratum of the *ātman*, the Knowledge undifferentiated. Thus, *jñāna* alone manifests as the multifarious *vijñāna*, while the *vijñāna* resolves in the *jñāna*. Thus, every act of knowing is *vijñāna*, while the source of all that knowledge is *jñāna*. We talk of this difference only from the standpoint of the apparent plurality. The Reality, from its own standpoint, is always One and non-dual. There is plurality from the point of view of manifestation, but It is one solid block of indivisible and undivided Awareness from the point of view of its source.

In the Upaniṣads, the non-dual nature of the Reality is repeatedly emphasized, because there is duality experienced day in and day out by the seeker. The human tendency is to take this plurality experienced through the senses and the mind as real. This powerful orientation of the mind is sought to be firmly neutralized by presenting the Oneness of the Reality from different standpoints.

सर्वं जगदिदं त्वत्तो जायते । सर्वं जगदिदं त्वत्तस्तिष्ठति । सर्वं जगदिदं त्वयि लयमेष्यति । सर्वं जगदिदं त्वयि प्रत्येति ।।

sarvaṁ jagadidaṁ tvatto jāyate ꟾ sarvaṁ jagadidaṁ tvattastiṣṭhati ꟾ sarvaṁ jagadidaṁ tvayi layameṣyati ı sarvaṁ jagadidaṁ tvayi pratyeti ıı

This entire universe originates from You. It exists because of (in) You. It will eventually resolve in You. This entire universe will finally become one with You.

The universe consists of countless phenomena. But, it is essentially described as a combination of three fundamental phenomena, namely, creation, sustenance and annihilation. The universe is always pointed out as *idam*, this. However great or valuable or marvellous a given object in the universe may be, it still becomes "this" to a conscious being. This alertness on the part of the seeker towards the "this-ness" of the universe is essential to develop a discrimination between the seen and the seer. Further, the universe is an effect, since every object of the universe, small and big, including stars and galaxies, and the universe itself, have origin in time. The effect must be preceded by the cause.

The cause of the universe is two-fold: material and efficient. The efficient cause is absolutely indispensable to the universe because the universe is very orderly, intelligently put together, symmetric and beautiful. It is naive to assume that the material has organized itself in the form of the universe as the *sāṅkhya*s and atheists do. The efficient cause is necessarily a conscious being. Thus the universe presupposes a Creator, who is a Conscious Being. The first statement in this *mantra* declares that *Brahman* called Gaṇapati is the cause of this universe. But, it does not specifically mention the nature of the cause. However, at this point of the *mantra*, we can take *Brahman*, the Conscious Being, as the efficient cause of the universe, like the pot maker for the pot.

But, then we need material for the creation of the universe. The second statement declaring that the universe continues to exist in *Brahman* makes it abundantly clear that none other than *Brahman* is the material cause of the universe, since the effect continues to exist in the material cause alone. The effect has no independent existence other than the existence of the material. The conclusion that *Brahman* is the material cause is further clinched in the third and fourth statements which declare that the universe in the end resolves in *Brahman* alone. Any effect finally has to resolve in its material. Thus these statements establish *Brahman* as the material-cum-efficient cause of the universe. Just as waves exist in water and ornaments in gold, this universe exists in *Brahman*. At the time of annihilation, the universe is withdrawn into *Brahman*.

Brahman as the material-cum-efficient cause of the universe is tenable only if: (1) *Brahman* is the Awareness-Existence, and (2) the universe is an appearance and hence unreal. An illustration of this unique situation is the dream. The conscious being, the dreamer, is both the efficient cause as well as the material out of which the dream world is created. If the universe were real, *Brahman* can, at best, be the efficient cause alone, and then the material remains unaccounted for. Also, the outside material makes *Brahman* (the unlimited) limited, which is a logical fallacy.

Here the annihilation is presented in two stages. In the first stage called *laya*, the entire universe gets resolved into its basic principles — the five subtle elements, the universal intelligence called *mahat* and the unmanifest seed (*māyā*) of the universe. In the final stage, called *pralaya*, everything including the unmanifest seed resolves into the non-dual *Brahman*. The prefix *pra* means total. In the first stage also, the substratum of resolution is *Brahman* alone, since these principles do not exist outside *Brahman*. They are invoked in the non-dual *Brahman* alone to account for the apparent differentiation of the universe.

Human nature always endeavours to seek a cause for every phenomenon in the creation. This notion of causation together with the notions of time and of space is the major obstacle in the realization of the Supreme Reality. There is only one ultimate cause which is *Brahman*. Other causes within the creation really do not matter. The only cause for every scene on the movie screen is the illuminated screen alone; seeking a cause for a given scene on the basis of an earlier scene is futile. The idea of causation is so deeply ingrained in the human psyche that it can only be neutralized by realizing that *Brahman* alone is the cause of all phenomena in the universe.

त्वं भूमिरापोऽनलोऽनिलो नभः ।

tvaṁ bhūmirāpo'nalo'nilo nabhaḥ ।

You are the earth, the waters, fire, air and space.

It is concluded from the previous discussion that *Brahman* alone manifests as this universe without undergoing any modifications. The reality of every scene on the screen is the illuminated screen alone. In the same way, the reality of this entire universe is *Brahman* alone. For the ease of understanding, we can interpose a step between the apparent world and the Reality. This entire world can be reduced to five basic elements. As long as we look at the world as consisting of objects and people, the mind will continue to project likes and dislikes. This world-centric vision is *saṁsāra*, and the worldliness is what mars our happiness. When we shift the focus from names and forms to the basic elements just short of the ultimate cause, the likes and dislikes will be diluted to a large extent, and the Reality will start to gloriously manifest in life.

The five basic elements do not differ in their content which is the Existence Absolute. The difference is only in the grossness or subtleness of the manifestation of this Existence. Thus the five elements listed in this *mantra* are all nothing but the Existence Absolute with gradually diminishing grossness. Existence in its grossest form is the earth, and in its subtlest form space, and the other three elements occupy the positions in between the two. Thus, in the vision of the enlightened person, the entire universe is reduced to the Supreme Reality through the intervening basic elements. Such a vision liberates the person from the thraldom of worldliness.

The five basic elements are indeed *Brahman*. The earth sustains life. This power is endowed to the earth by *Brahman* alone, as it is declared in the *Gītā* (15-13) by the Lord:

गामाविश्य च भूतानि धारयाम्यहमोजसा ।

gāmāviśya ca bhūtāni dhārayāmyahamojasā ।

I enter the earth and I sustain the living beings with my power.

Similarly, water with its power to quench the thirst and sustain life is a marvellous manifestation of the Lord. This is the spirit behind the worship of the rivers like the Gaṅgā, the Yamunā, the Godāvarī, etc., in India. Fire is the foremost altar recommended by the Vedas for worshipping the Lord. As we have already seen, the directly experienced form (*pratyakṣam*) of *Brahman* is air. Space is equally the manifestation of the Lord and is worshipped as such in Chidambaram of south India. In Chidambaram, space is the altar in which the Lord is worshipped. All offerings are made to the invisible space-*liṅga* (symbol) of the Lord Śiva. The *Taittirīyopaniṣad* (1-6) describes space as the physical body of *Brahman*.

आकाशशरीरं ब्रह्म ।

ākāśaśarīraṁ brahma ।

Brahman has the space as Its body.

We should not misunderstand that *Brahman* has transformed into these five elements. That would make *Brahman* a material object subject to modification and hence unreal. *Brahman* is not the transformational cause of the five elements; It is the apparitional cause. *Brahman* continues to be what It is, Existence Absolute, even though It is the substratum of the universe which is an appearance. The appearance which is unreal can in no way affect *Brahman*. Earth, water, etc., are different names of the same Existence Absolute.

त्वं चत्वारि वाक् (परिमिता) पदानि ।

tvaṁ catvāri vāk (parimitā) padāni ।

You are the speech limited to four kinds of words.

A speciality of the Hindu scriptures is that every aspect of life in this creation is very vividly described. One example is the faculty of speech. It is pertinent to quote here a hymn from the *Ṛgveda* (1.164.45) to explain this statement about the power of speech as the manifestation of the Lord:

चत्वारि वाक् परिमिता पदानि तानि विदुर्ब्राह्मणा ये मनीषिण: ।
गुहा त्रीणि निहिता नेङ्गयन्ति तुरीयं वाचो मनुष्या वदन्ति ॥

catvāri vāk parimitā padāni tāni vidur brāhmaṇā ye manīṣiṇaḥ ।

guhā trīṇi nihitā neṅgayanti turīyaṁ vāco manuṣyā vadanti ॥

The speech is limited to four-fold division. All the four divisions are known to scholars of the Vedas

who have realized the Self. Of the four, three are
hidden in the cave of the intellect. Common people
are unaware of those three. What they routinely
speak is the fourth variety.

Speech is four-fold and all the four kinds of speech are the
manifestation of the Universal Power alone. They do not
belong to the ego as is wrongly claimed by the ego (that is,
by us) due to ignorance. What are the four kinds of speech?
There are a number of answers to this question. One
possibility is that they could be the four primordial sounds
which were present at the time of creation itself. They are
oṁ, bhūḥ, bhuvaḥ and *suvaḥ*. These four sounds are related
to Vedic cosmology. Or they could be *nāma* (noun), *ākhyāta*
(verb), *upasarga* (preposition) and *nipāta* (indeclinable or
irregular). These are related to Vedic grammar. Or they
may be *mantra* (hymn), *kalpa* (rules of the Vedic rituals),
Brāhmaṇa (commentary on the hymns) and the vernacular
(speech of the common people). These are related to the
Vedic rituals (*adhidaiva*).

Or they can be the sounds of the domesticated animals,
the instruments like the kettledrum, etc., the wild animals
and the humans. These relate to the manifestation of the
Universal Power as life on earth, since the sounds of the
instruments are also caused by living beings. Or they can
be the sounds of the earth, the atmosphere (of the wind),
the interstellar space and the humans. The importance of
human beings in the scheme of things called creation is
noteworthy, as they occupy, in the vision of the Vedas, the
fourth slot together with earth, wind and space. These
categories belong to the physical universe (*adhibhūta*).

Or the four-fold sounds may be located in the body-
mind-sense complex of the individual (*adhyātma*). They are:
(i) *Parā*, the unmanifest and undifferentiated power of the
speech latent in the human being. This is located in the

base of the backbone, which is a power centre called *mūlādhāra*. (ii) *Paśyantī*, the same power coloured or differentiated by the specific emotion of the mind. As the person wishes to speak, the power travels upwards to another power centre located in the navel. It is called *maṇipūra*. There it gets associated with the emotion of the mind. (iii) *Madhyamā*, the same power which has acquired the form of a specific word by association with the intellect which is the determinative faculty. This transformation takes place as the power enters the higher power centre, the heart which is called *anāhata*. (iv) *Vaikharī*, the final spoken word. As the above power enters the power centre in the throat called *viśuddhi*, it acquires the form of a spoken word. Thus every thought and every spoken word is the glory of the Universal Power reflected in the physico-psychic apparatus called the individual. It is obvious that the fourth manifestation of the power, the spoken word, alone is known to the common people. The other three can be recognized only by students of yogic practices.

In Telugu, there is a proverb to the effect that, when a person speaks the truth, it originates from the navel, and if he is speaking an untruth, he is speaking from the lips. I came across a speech therapist examining a person who was unable to speak properly due to a problem of pain in the throat. The therapist advised him to speak deliberately from the navel, and not from the throat. This advice was found to be very effective in reducing the throat pain of people in the teaching profession and others, who have to speak for long durations. Even while speaking, I am the witness of my speech. Therefore, it is advisable, while giving a lecture, etc., to contemplate that the sound comes from the navel and not from the throat. It is a way to relax the throat.

The Thousand Names of the Universal Power (*Lalitā-*

sahasra-nāma) lists these four kinds of speech as the forms
of the Universal Mother, Lalitā :

परा प्रत्यक् चितीरूपा पश्यन्ती परदेवता ।

मध्यमा वैखरीरूपा – (१३२)

parā pratyakcitīrūpā paśyantī paradevatā ।
madhyamā vaikharīrūpā — (132)

The Universal Mother obtaining as the Awareness
Absolute manifests as the four forms of speech, *parā*,
paśyantī, *madhyamā* and *vaikharī*.

त्वं गुणत्रयातीत: ।

tvaṁ guṇatrayātītaḥ ।

You transcend the three *guṇa*s (of the *māyā-
śakti*).

Vedāntic cosmogony (theory of the origin of the universe)
postulates that the Creative Power (*māyā-śakti*) of *Brahman*,
out of which this universe has emanated, is constituted by
three *guṇa*s (constituents of the Power), *sattva*, *rajas* and
tamas. This universe constituting both the sentient and the
insentient can be reduced to three fundamental principles,
matter, energy and consciousness. Every entity in this
universe is a manifestation of one, two or all of these three
principles in different permutations and combinations. The
nature of the effect is determined by the characteristics of
the cause. Hence, there must be three constituents in the
cause of the universe to account for this three-fold manifestation, which is indeed the case. They are the three *guṇa*s
of the Unmanifest : the *sattva*, *rajas* and *tamas*. Thus this
entire universe is a combination of these three *guṇa*s in
different proportions, while the substratum of the existence
is *Brahman*. This is beautifully explained by the Lord in a
verse of the *Gītā* (18-40) :

न तदस्ति पृथिव्यां वा दिवि देवेषु वा पुन: ।
सत्त्वं प्रकृतिजैर्मुक्तं यदेभिस्स्यात् त्रिभिर्गुणै: ॥

na tadasti pṛthivyāṁ vā divi deveṣu vā punaḥ ।
sattvaṁ prakṛtijairmuktaṁ yadebhissyāt tribhirguṇaiḥ ॥

There is not a single thing on the earth, or in the
heavens, or in the gods, which is devoid of these
three *guṇa*s of the Nature (*māyā-śakti*).

When *Brahmaṇ*, the Existence-Awareness Absolute, is
manifest in *sattva*, consciousness unfolds; when manifest
in *rajas*, energy and activity issues forth; when manifest in
tamas, matter originates. We understand that *Brahman* is
the apparitional, and not the transformational, cause of
the universe; hence the universe is unreal. It, therefore,
becomes obvious that *Brahman* Itself is neither contaminated
nor affected by these *guṇa*s, because *Brahman* is the Absolute
Reality, while the *guṇa*s belong to the empirical reality. This
is the vision relating to the *adhibhūta* (the physical universe).

Now, let us look at the *adhyātma* (the individual). There
are the three fundamental moods of the mind. They are :
(i) the mind is alert gaining knowledge of the things of the
world, (ii) it is vagrant and restless, and (iii) it is languid,
having or showing disinclination for physical exertion.
These three moods of the mind are respectively caused by
the three *guṇa*s of the Unmanifest, *sattva*, *rajas* and *tamas*.
However, Awareness Absolute, the *ātman*, though
illuminating all these moods of the mind, is Itself not affected
in any way by these *guṇa*s. This glory of *ātman* is described
in the *Gītā* (14-22) by the Lord as follows:

प्रकाशं च प्रवृत्तिं च मोहमेव च पाण्डव ।
न द्वेष्टि संप्रवृत्तानि न निवृत्तानि काङ्क्षति ॥

prakāśaṁ ca pravṛttiṁ ca mohameva ca pāṇḍava ।
na dveṣṭi sampravṛttāni na nivṛttāni kāṅkṣati ॥

Knowledge is the result of *sattva*, activity the result
of *rajas* and delusion the result of *tamas*. When these
phenomena take place, the knower of the Self does
not hate them; when they disappear, he does not
hanker after them.

This description is about the knower of the Self. We should
note that there is absolutely no difference whatsoever
between the knower of the Self and the Lord.

Where are all the three *guṇas*? They are all located in
the mind, not in the *ātman*. When the mind is lazy, the
ātman illuminates the laziness of the mind. If the mind is
active, It illuminates that activity; and if the mind is in
harmony, It also illuminates that *sattva guṇa*. In fact, the
seekers of Self-knowledge are advised to keep the mind in
the *sattva guṇa*, because it is in that state that the true nature
of oneself can be readily appreciated. The mind in the *sattva*
readily resolves into the *ātman*. The mind in the *rajas* can
never resolve and the mind in the *tamas* resolves in the
insentient, and the individual becomes one with the body.
The mind in the *sattva* helps the seeker to appreciate the
Higher Truth which is his own essential nature. The Higher
Truth is not *sattva*; and neither is it *rajas* nor *tamas*; It is
ātman which illuminates all the three *guṇas* and yet, It
transcends all of them.

त्वं अवस्थात्रयातीतः ।

tvaṁ avasthātrayātītaḥ ।

You transcend all the three mental
experiences (of the waking, dream and deep
sleep).

The individual's life is a repeated succession of the cycle of
the three states of experience, namely, the sleep, dream and
waking. In the waking state, there are objects and their

perception. Then there is the dream state in which there is perception of objects without there being any objects. In sleep, there are neither objects nor their perception. However, there is also a certain experience in sleep as in the other two states. Sleep is not non-existence; it is an actual experience of joy and a general sense of well-being. There is a seed of consciousness in sleep. Though it is an experience of the absence of empirical world, the presence of the Absolute is experienced by all of us in the sleep, albeit without recognizing it.

In sleep we are all aware of not being conscious of the world. In the waking state, we are aware of being conscious of the world. In dream, we are aware of the dream world created by the mind. Each of these three states negates the other two, proving that all of them are time-bound and hence unreal. All the three states (*avasthās*) are illuminated by the Awareness. The essential content of any experience is the Awareness, just as the essential content of an ornament is gold, or that of a wave or even the absence of the wave is water.

But the *ātman* illuminating the three mental states is One non-negatable Existence-Awareness Absolute. It includes all the three states but transcends them. Time and space are only mental categories. They limit the mental modifications and also the things objectified by such ever-changing modifications. But, time and space do not limit the Awareness from which the universe together with time and space arises. That Awareness is called *ātman*, being the essential content of the individual. It is timeless and spaceless; It is beyond the illusory limitations of time and space. Hence, that Awareness is Infinite. This is the reason why the Upaniṣads declare that *ātman* is the same as *Brahman*.

तवं देहत्रयातीतः ।

tvaṁ dehatrayātītaḥ ।

You transcend all the three bodies.

The Infinite *ātman* is, as though, embedded or imprisoned in the individuality which is essentially a combination of three bodies. They are the gross body, the subtle body and the causal body. There is nothing physical or real about these bodies. It is not that *ātman* is really imprisoned in the physical body. On the other hand, it is the physical body that derives its existence and life from *ātman*. The individual, being ignorant of his own true nature, commits the mistake of taking the physical body as oneself. This mistake alone binds one to the physical body. But, the physical body has its existence in the mind, since there is a physical body (the notion of my body or me) only when one thinks of it. This wrong thought, repeated endlessly, is the subtle body imprisoning the Infinite.

The body belongs to the person; the person is nothing but the thread of habits and memories, a bundle of fears and cravings, entirely the creature of the mind. Person is not the real subject, but he or she masquerades as the subject. The particular or the part called the person is never separate from the whole or the universal. In fact, all the three, viz., the sense of being a limited person, the physical body and the world arise from and resolve into the Awareness simultaneously.

This person (the subtle body) and the physical body are absent in the sleep. They arise from the seed of ignorance which is one of the characteristics of sleep. Sleep is characterized by the common experience that, "I slept happily without knowing anything." As the sleep comes to an end, and the mind comes into existence as a motion in the infinite ocean of Awareness, a sense of separate existence is projected by habit and the life of *saṁsāra* begins. This habit of taking oneself to be separate from the whole is the sprout of ignorance. It is called the causal body, since it is the origin of the other two bodies when one wakes up. As the person sleeps, the physical body resolves in the subtle body, which in turn resolves in the causal body, namely the fundamental sense of separate existence.

Thus the bodily existence, the person and the fundamental sense of separate existence are only movements in the infinite ocean of Awareness (*cit*). These are unreal because they are negated all the time. Only the unreal gets negated. In and through all these bodies shines the light of *cit*, which is their only Reality. The waking state is characterized by the identification with the physical body, while the dream state entirely belongs to the subtle body, the mind. The causal body belongs to the state of deep sleep. Each of these bodies is an experience, and the Awareness Infinite is the only essential content of both the experience and the experiencer.

तवं कालत्रयातीतः ।

tvaṁ kālatrayātītaḥ ।

You transcend all the three divisions of time.

The concept of time is very subtle and interesting. The understanding of time in terms of the past, present and future is a property of mind and it does not exist outside the person. Thought is invariably associated with time and it is against the time-space framework that every thought arises. Time is the mental awareness of the sequence of the events based on memory. Or, we can say that time is the consciousness of the motion of a body in space. Both the memory of the past and the imagination about the future are events that occur in the present and therefore the past and future are "now." There is no event or thing which is not in the eternal "now." The division of time is purely a categorization by the mind. Once the division of time is negated, time itself gets negated.

The present or "now," is itself not different from "I am," or from the consciousness. Present is not today, since a part of today has already gone by and the remaining part is yet to come. Present is not even this hour; not even this minute, since a minute is made up of sixty seconds. Even a second can be subdivided into milli-, micro-, nano-, pico-second, etc. We can simply say that the present is the briefest possible present moment. What is the truth of such a moment? If you carefully examine the present moment within yourself, you will recognize that it is not different from the conscious presence "I am" which itself is a whirlpool in the ocean of Awareness Absolute which is the Infinite *ātman*.

The moment you examine the present moment, it resolves in you. Time being a property of the mind and an important component of thought, there is no time in the silence of the mind between two thoughts. That is why there is no apprehension of time in sleep. In meditation, there would be no awareness of the passage of time if your thoughts could resolve in the *ātman*, the Awareness. In the joyful state of laughter, the mind gets resolved in its source and hence, there is no time in pure joy. The mind along with the categories of time and space arises in the *ātman*, and resolves in the *ātman*. Thus *ātman* alone is the substratum and Reality of the mind and its categories. Therefore the *ātman* transcends time and its divisions. Thus, you, the *ātman*, are truly timeless. Timelessness does not mean extending into the endless flow of time; time-lessness means transcending time, that is, going beyond the illusion of time.

As an example, we may say that gold transcends the necklace; in the reality of gold, there is no necklace. As long as a person takes the time to be real, he is stuck with regrets and guilt of the past, and constantly reaches out into the future with trepidation. When the person overcomes this hypnosis of time and learns to live in the eternal present, the door to his innermost Reality which is *Brahman* opens up and the bondage of *saṁsāra* (worldliness) and the cycle of birth and death come to an end.

त्वं मूलाधारस्थितोऽसि नित्यम् ।

tvaṁ mūlādhārasthito'si nityam ।

You always abide in the base of the spine.

We should not look upon the human body as merely an assemblage of the flesh, blood, bones, etc. It is a power house where the mysterious power of the Lord reflects. The body is very appropriately described in the *Gītā* (13-1) as a field, *kṣetra*. It is the field of consciousness from which all kinds of power arise. This infinite universal power of the Lord, while reflecting in the physical body, has a concentrated presence in specific parts of the body called *cakra*s (centres of power). They are sequentially as follows : the base of the back-bone called *mūlādhāra*, the abdomen called *svādhiṣṭhāna*, the navel called *maṇipūra*, the heart called *anāhata*, the throat called *viśuddhi*, the centre of the eye-brows called *ājñā* and the brain called *sahasrāra*. The most basic of them is the *mūlādhāra*, and the devotees visualize the Lord there in meditation.

The Lord is all-pervading and everything and every place exists in the Lord alone. However, for the purpose of fixing the vagrant mind to an anchor, the devotee may visualize the Lord in any aspect of the creation, for example the sun, the moon, ocean, rivers, mountains, trees, etc., which particularly expresses the glory of the Lord. This is the spirit of the Hindus worshipping the Lord in myriad forms. The Lord can be visualized in life forms such as a peepal tree, a cow, a Vedic scholar, the parents or the teacher. This way the mind is always in the sacred presence of the Lord and the visualization of Divinity becomes easy. Similarly, the all-pervading Lord can be worshipped in the shrine of a temple. The Lord may be visualized by directing the mind inwards, and fixed to a given form or a *mantra* or even a power centre described earlier as the *cakra*. But the devotee should not forget that the Lord is all-pervading and that such a visualization is meant for the purpose of controlling the fickleness of the mind alone. To believe that the Lord is really fixed to a spot or to a thing or to a centre is a mockery of Truth. Such a belief does not serve the devotee well in the long run.

त्वं शक्तित्रयात्मकः ।।

tvaṁ śaktitrayātmakaḥ ।।

You alone manifest as the three-fold power.

We should look at the universe, not as a collection of different objects, but as a marvellous manifestation of the Infinite Power of the Lord. The matter is condensed energy and consciousness is a very subtle kind of power. The Lord creates this universe out of his own Power (*māyā-śakti*). The phenomenon called universe can be divided into three sub-phenomena : creation, sustenance and annihilation. Accordingly, we visualize the Lord as the source of the three-fold power of creation, sustenance and annihilation. This concept is beautifully explained in the following verse of *Śrīmadbhāgavatam* (4-9-7) :

एकस्त्वमेव भगवन्निदमात्मशक्त्या मायाख्ययोरुगुणया महदाद्यशेषम् ।
सृष्ट्वानुविश्य पुरुषस्तदसद्गुणेषु नानेव दारुषु विभावसुवद्विभासि ।।

ekastvameva bhagavannidamātmaśaktyā māyākhyayo-
ruguṇayā mahadādyaśeṣam ।
sṛṣṭvānuviśya puruṣastadasadguṇeṣu nāneva dāruṣu
vibhāvasuvadvibhāsi ॥

O Lord, You are the One Infinite *Brahman* that
created this universal intelligence down to the
physical universe with your own three-fold (*sattva,*
rajas, and *tamas*) Power (*māyā-śakti*). Having created
the universe, you entered it (as Existence and
Awareness) and you alone shine in the unreal names
and forms of the universe, just like the sole fire in a
number of burning pieces of wood.

That was the *adhibhūta* aspect of the three-fold power. Now,
let us see the *adhyātma* aspect of the same three-fold power.
The Infinite Power of the Lord reflects in this physico-
psychic apparatus called human being, making him or her
a live conscious being. This expression of the Lord's power
is once again three-fold: the power of desiring, the power
of knowing and the power of acting (life). In this respect,
all life forms are alike. However, the first two powers are
particularly potent in human beings, while in the lower
life forms of flora and fauna, the power of life is the
prominent one, the other two being dormant. The so-called
jīva (individual) should realize that the ideas of "me" and
"mine" with reference to these powers is a distortion of
truth, since these powers entirely belong to the Lord. Once
again, this point is beautifully highlighted in the following
verse of *Śrīmadbhāgavatam* (4-9-6):

योऽन्तः प्रविश्य मम वाचमिमां प्रसुप्तां सञ्जीवयत्यखिलशक्तिधरस्स्वधाम्ना ।
अन्यांश्च हस्तचरणश्रवणत्वगादीन् प्राणान्नमो भगवते पुरुषाय तुभ्यम् ॥

yo'ntaḥ praviśya mama vācamimāṁ prasuptāṁ sañjīva-
yatyakhilaśaktidharassvadhāmnā ।

*anyāṁśca   hastacaraṇaśravaṇatvagādīn   prāṇānnamo
bhagavate puruṣāya tubhyam* ॥

The Cosmic Person, wielding infinite power, entered
in me and brought to life this otherwise dormant
faculty of speech and also other organs like hands,
legs, ears, skin, etc. My prostrations, O Lord, unto
you.

The three-fold Power of the Lord is also called Lalitā. This
glory of the Lord's Power in *adhyātma* is nicely brought out
in one of the thousand names of Lalitā in the *Lalitā-sahasra-
nāma* (181) :

इच्छाशक्तिज्ञानशक्तिक्रियाशक्तिस्वरूपिणी ॥

icchāśaktijñānaśaktikriyāśaktisvarūpiṇī ॥

The three-fold powers of desiring, knowing and
acting are the manifestations of the Universal
Mother.

With reference to the power of desiring, we should note
that as long as such a power is exercised in accordance
with *dharma* (the Laws of Nature), it is in harmony with
the Whole. But, when the same power is in conflict with
the Whole, it becomes the cause of suffering here or
hereafter. The Lord says thus in the *Gītā* (7-11):

धर्माऽविरुद्धो भूतेषु कामोऽस्मि भरतर्षभ ॥

dharmā'viruddho bhūteṣu kāmo'smi bharatarṣabha ॥

O Arjuna, In the living beings I am the desire, which
is not against the Nature's order.

From this analysis, it is clear that the One Supreme Reality
is known by different names such as Gaṇapati, Śrīhari,
Nārāyaṇa, Śrī Kṛṣṇa, Lalitā, Brahmā, etc.

त्वां योगिनो ध्यायन्ति नित्यम् ।

tvāṁ yogino dhyāyanti nityam ।

*Yogī*s contemplate upon you all the time.

Yogī is the one who seeks communion or identity with the Lord. Such a seeker relates to the Lord, particularly in the form of Gaṇapati at all times and in all places. We are virtually dwelling in the lap of the Lord, since the entire universe is the manifestation of the Lord alone. Abiding with such a prayerful attitude in all the activities of life is called *yoga*, since such a lifestyle connects the individual with the Whole. Generally, people live in the world-consciousness. The seeker is advised to live instead in the Divine Consciousness, and carry on with the affairs of the world. If only we look for the Lord, He is everywhere. He is both within and without, as pointed out in the *Mahānārāyaṇopaniṣad* (13).

अन्तर्बहिश्च तत्सर्वं व्याप्य नारायणस्थित: ।।

antarbahiśca tatsarvaṁ vyāpya nārāyaṇassthitaḥ ।।

The Lord Nārāyaṇa pervades everything, both within and without.

The lotus leaf, even while remaining all the time in the murky water, neither becomes wet, nor dirty. Worldly life is inevitable for everybody including the renunciates. But, a person who conducts his worldly affairs with an attitude of "generous non-attachment" and takes precautions against emotional dependence on the objects of pleasure and relationships in the world is called a *yogī*. For such a seeker, constant communion with the Lord is normal.

त्वं ब्रह्मा त्वं विष्णुस्त्वं रुद्रस्त्वमिन्द्रस्त्वमग्निस्त्वं वायुस्त्वं सूर्यस्त्वं
चन्द्रमास्त्वं ब्रह्म भूर्भुवस्सुवरोम् ॥ ६ ॥

tvaṁ brahmā tvaṁ viṣṇustvaṁ rudrastvamindrastvamagnistvaṁ vāyustvaṁ sūryastvaṁ
candramāstvaṁ brahma bhūrbhuvassuvarom ॥
6 ॥

You are Brahmā; You are Viṣṇu; You are
Rudra; You are Indra; You are Agni; You are
Vāyu; You are Sūrya; You are Candra; You are
All; You are the utterances (or the *lokas*) *bhūḥ*,
bhuvaḥ, *suvaḥ* and *om* (the *Brahman*).

The Cosmic Power, which is the source of this creation,
and which sustains this creation, can be viewed from many
aspects. It is given a particular name corresponding to each
of Its aspects. For example, the Lord associated with the
power of creation is called Brahmājī; the Lord associated
with the power of sustenance is called Viṣṇu; and the Lord
associated with the power of annihilation is called Rudra.
Each aspect of that Infinite Cosmic Power is visualized as a
god. Thus, all the gods may be viewed as the many limbs of
the Lord. There are eight gods as the overlords of the eight
quarters. Of them, a few are mentioned in this *mantra*. They
are Indra, the god of physical prowess; Agni, the god of
fire; and Vāyu, the god of wind. The Sun and the Moon are
also important manifestations of the Cosmic Power of the
Lord. Thus everything in this creation is a manifestation of
the Lord alone. Even the primordial sounds of creation are
the manifestations of that Cosmic Power of the Lord alone.

If we examine any Vedic ritual, we hear names of
different gods. This constant repetition of different names
may make the devotee believe that plurality is real. Hence,

the scriptures constantly exhort the devotee that the plurality of gods is only in the names by which they are addressed in prayer. The Reality is One. The One appears as the all, and the all are in the One. The spirit of the Vedic vision is Unity. The diversity of names and forms is only an empirical reality. Such a diversity is not only accepted, but also welcomed, as it only glorifies the One Reality. In this context, we may remember the famous statement of the *Ṛgveda* (1-164-46) :

इन्द्रं मित्रं वरुणमग्निमाहुरथो दिव्यस्स सुपर्णो गरुत्मान् ।

एकं सद्विप्रा बहुधा वदन्त्यग्निं यमं मातरिश्वानमाहुः ॥

indraṁ   mitraṁ   varuṇamagnimāhuratho   divyassa
suparṇo garutmān ।
ekaṁ   sadviprā   bahudhā   vadantyagniṁ   yamaṁ
mātariśvānamāhuḥ ॥

This Infinite *ātman*, the Supreme Reality, the Existence Absolute is One. But, the seers call it by different names such as Indra, Mitra, Varuṇa, Suparṇa (the divine eagle), Garutmān, Agni, Yama and Mātariśvan.

If we are not alert to this unity, the vagrant nature of the mind remains intact even after worshipping the Lord for a long time. A wandering mind cannot appreciate the Higher Truth. According to the Vedic cosmology, the universe is divided into three *loka*s or levels of existence. They are *bhūḥ* (terrestrial), *bhuvaḥ* (intermediate), and *suvaḥ* (celestial). It is obvious that the Lord alone is in the form of these *loka*s. These three worlds arise from the corresponding primordial sounds *bhūḥ*, *bhuvaḥ*, and *suvaḥ* respectively. These sounds represent the Will of the Lord to create the three-fold universe.

गणादिं पूर्वमुच्चार्य वर्णादींस्तदनन्तरम् । अनुस्वारः परतरः ।

अर्धेन्दुलसितम् । तारेण ऋद्धम् । एतत्तव मनुस्वरूपम् ॥ ७ ॥

*gaṇādiṁ pūrvamuccārya varṇādīṁstada-
nantaram ı anusvāraḥ parataraḥ ı ardhendulasitam ı tāreṇa ṛddham ı etattava manusvarūpam
॥ 7 ॥*

The first syllable of the word *gaṇa*, that is, *g*, has to be pronounced first, followed by the first of the vowels. That has to be followed by the *anusvāra* (the sound *ṁ*), embellished by the crescent of the moon (which represents the nasal sound). All this has to be made auspicious (or more powerful) by pronouncing the sacred sound *om* (in the beginning). This is the true description of Your *mantra*.

Here, the teacher gives a detailed description of the Gaṇapati *mantra*. It is simply *oṁ gam*. It is a one-syllabled *mantra*. In the script, the half crescent on the top of the syllable indicates that the sound is nasal. The sacred sound *om* is called *tāra*, for two reasons. Firstly, it is a prolonged sound (four units of time) like the sound of a bell (one unit of time is the time taken to pronounce a short vowel like *a*). Secondly, it helps the seeker to resolve his little self in the *ātman* which is the source of all sounds, all activities and all knowledge, thereby liberating him or her from the life of "becoming."

Here we find an elaborate description of the one-syllabled *mantra*. The elaboration is significant. The human body is made up of different limbs like hands and legs or different kinds of tissues like blood, muscle and fat. But, we should not think that the form of the Lord is similar to human form. The form of the essentially formless Lord can be that of the *mantra* itself. Therefore, different syllables of the *mantra* are like different limbs of the Lord's form. Consider the following verse from *Śrīmadbhāgavatam* (1-5-38), which explains this concept of the Lord's form :

इति मूर्त्यभिधानेन मन्त्रमूर्तिममूर्तिकम् ।
यजते यज्ञपुरुषं स सम्यग्दर्शनः पुमान् ।।

*iti mūrtyabhidhānena mantramūrtimamūrtikam ı yajate
yajñapuruṣaṁ sa samyagdarśanaḥ pumān ॥*

The Lord, who is in the form of Vedic rituals, is essentially formless; yet the *mantra* is His form. The one who worships the Lord in a given form through the *mantra* while knowing Him thus is the one who has correct understanding of the Lord.

गकारः पूर्वरूपम् । अकारो मध्यमरूपम् । अनुस्वारश्चान्त्यरूपम् ।
बिन्दुरुत्तररूपम् । नादस्संधानम् । सग्ंहिता संधिः ।। ८ ।।

*gakāraḥ pūrvarūpam ı akāro madhyamarūpam ı
anusvāraścāntyarūpam ı binduruttararūpam ı
nādassandhānam ı saṁhitā sandhiḥ ॥ 8 ॥*

The first syllable is *g*, the middle syllable *a*, and the last syllable is *m*. The last syllable progresses into a nasal sound called *bindu*, and is further pulled into a lengthy sound called *nāda*, which unites all these parts into a *mantra*. All these individual sounds are pronounced sequentially in unison (*saṁhitā*), when the *mantra* is complete.

Further elaboration of the simple *mantra* continues. The *mantra* is divided into various parts. It is visualized as

consisting of five parts as described above. The vivid
description is very useful in providing a support system for
the vacillating mind. Mind needs, as it were, a peg to hold
on to. Any form of the Lord, depending upon one's personal
preference, can serve such a purpose. A sound symbol is
even better, since it is our common experience that it is easier
to concentrate the mind on a given sound than on a given
form. A form is too fickle for the mind to hold on to,
whereas a sound seems quite "solid" for the mind to hold
on. In addition to this tangible rationale, there is also a
deeper esoteric significance associated with the *mantra*.

The prolonged sound, *nāda*, described above serves a
wonderful purpose in meditation. It launches, as it were,
the mind into silence by effectively putting an end to the
thoughts. Thus, the *nāda* serves to resolve the small self into
the Awareness Absolute. If we are attentive to this *nāda*
and the subsequent silence, we can hear the profound
silence. We can then also recognize that all sounds, all
activity and all knowledge emanate from that silent
Awareness. This Awareness, the source of all sounds, which
one reaches through the *nāda* is sometimes called *nāda-
brahman*. Even the classical musicians of India demonstrate
this *nāda* in their concerts.

सैषा गणेशविद्या । गणक ऋषिः । निचृद्गायत्रीच्छन्दः ।
गणपतिर्देवता । ओम्, गं गणपतये नमः ॥ ९ ॥

*saiṣā gaṇeśavidyā ı gaṇaka ṛṣih ı nicṛdgāyatrī-
chandaḥ ı gaṇapatirdevatā ı om, gaṁ gaṇapataye
namaḥ* ıı 9 ıı

This is the mental worship of the Lord
Gaṇapati. The seer of this *mantra* is Gaṇaka.
The metre is *nicṛdgāyatrī*. The presiding deity

is Gaṇapati. Oṁ gam, my prostrations unto the
Lord Gaṇapati.

The mental worship (upāsanā) with the support of a mantra
is called vidyā. In a different context, vidyā also means the
knowledge of the Self. Every mantra is a revelation to, or
the realization of, a seer. A saintly person of pure heart
withdraws from the affairs of the world and abides in the
ātman. It is then that the knowledge which is not sensorial,
mental or empirical manifests in that heart. Thus, this
knowledge is inspirational rather than intellectual. It is not
sullied by likes, dislikes or other limitations of the small
person (ego). It is not the knowledge created by the person.
It is the knowledge that takes place when the person is
resolved in the Whole. That is why it is called the knowledge
of the Lord or the knowledge revealed by the Lord. Such a
saintly person is called ṛṣi. In the present context, Gaṇaka
is the ṛṣi. I have a feeling that he may have had another
name, but probably owing to his discovery of this mantra,
he came to be known as Gaṇaka. In my opinion scientists
like Newton, Einstein are also seers, as their discoveries are
universal in scope. At the time of such a discovery, the ego
of the scientist gets resolved in the ātman, and in that sense,
such a discovery is indeed divine and not personal or man-
made.

Empirical knowledge, or the information generated by
man is time-bound. It begins at a particular time and ends
at another time. But the knowledge related to the Real is
timeless. It had no beginning and it will not come to an
end. Such knowledge is never created, but only discovered.
This discussion of the revealed knowledge applies equally
to the mantras related to mental worship. Here the single-
syllabled mantra which was described earlier in detail, is
further integrated into a longer eight-syllabled (without

counting the *om*) *mantra*. This *mantra*, popularly known as *mahā* Gaṇapati *mantra*, is widely believed to be very powerful in eliminating the obstacles that the devotees face in their day-to-day life. In addition, the *mantra* also removes obstructions in the devotees' efforts to purify their hearts and prepare them for the higher knowledge of the Self.

There is a scriptural injunction that the seeker should remember details about any *mantra* that he is going to recite, such as the meter, the presiding deity etc. The *Chāndogyopaniṣad* (1-3-9,10) prescribes these details in the following way :

– यदार्षेयं तमृषिं यां देवतामभिष्टोष्यन् स्यात्तां देवतामुपधावेत् ।
येन च्छन्दसा स्तोष्यन् स्यात्तच्छन्द उपधावेत् – ॥

– *yadarṣeyaṁ tamṛṣiṁ yāṁ devatāmabhiṣṭoṣyan syāttāṁ devatāmupadhāvet*ı *yena cchandasā stoṣyan syāttacchanda upadhāvet* –

The devotee should reflect on the seer who realized the *mantra*, and also on the presiding deity eulogized in the *mantra*. The devotee may also reflect on the meter in which the *mantra* is set.

एकदन्ताय विद्महे वक्रतुण्डाय धीमहि । तन्नो दन्तिः प्रचोदयात्
॥ १० ॥

*ekadantāya vidmahe vakratuṇḍāya dhīmahi*ı
tanno dantiḥ pracodayāt ॥ 10 ॥

We know Lord Gaṇapati and contemplate upon Him. He has only one tusk and his trunk is curved. In that contemplation, may the Lord Gaṇapati inspire our thoughts.

This *mantra* is called *gaṇapati gāyatrī*, since it is set in the *gāyatrī* meter. The meter *gāyatrī* has a very special place in the Vedic literature. The *Ṛgveda*, the foremost of the Vedas, begins with this metre. There is invariably a *mantra* in this metre for every form of the Lord. We find a string of such *mantras* in the *Mahānārāyaṇopaniṣad* (1). This *mantra* is also found there with a slight variation. The metre *gāyatrī* is so popular and important in the Vedic literature that Lord Śrī Kṛṣṇa declared in the *Gītā* (10-35) that among the metres, *gāyatrī* is Himself.

गायत्री च्छन्दसामहम् ।

gāyatrī cchandasāmaham ।

I am the *gāyatrī* among the metres.

The tenor of this prayer is very interesting. The devotee does not present any desire before the Lord. He recognizes that every thought has its origin in *ātman*, which is not different from the Lord. Also, thoughts just take place; they follow the laws of Nature. They are not controlled by the small self. In fact, the small self is itself no more than a thought. In that recognition, he prays to the Lord to inspire his thoughts with devotion to Him and bestow upon him the knowledge of the Self.

The form of the Lord as Gaṇapati is very popular among the Hindus. I once came across a very interesting incident. In Nashville, Tennesse, USA, the local Hindus wanted to build a temple. After much debate about the form of the Lord to be consecrated in the temple, the choice was narrowed down to Lord Veṅkaṭeśvara and Lord Gaṇapati. Then voting was held among the members of the community, and 80 per cent of the people voted for the Lord Gaṇapati. It was an interesting poll, as the winner and the loser were the same Lord. The Lord's form of Gaṇapati is elaborately described in the Purāṇas such as the *Gaṇeśa Purāṇa* and the *Śiva Purāṇa*. There is an interesting symbolism in this form of the Lord. The *Maudgala*

Purāṇa describes this form of the Lord as the *saguṇa* (with attributes) *Brahman* :

एकशब्दात्मिका माया तस्यास्सर्वं समुद्भवम् ।

दन्तस्सत्ताधरस्तत्र मायाचालक उच्यते ।

तयोर्योगे गणेशोऽयमेकदन्तः प्रकीर्तितः ।।

ekaśabdātmikā māyā tasyāssarvaṁ samudbhavam ।
dantassattādharastatra māyācālaka ucyate ।
tayoryoge gaṇeśo'yamekadantaḥ prakīrtitaḥ ।।

The word *eka* stands for the *māyā-śakti* from which this entire universe has originated. The word *danta* means the Existence Absolute that is *Brahman* which has this *māyā-śakti* in Its absolute control. Gaṇeśa, a combination of the above two principles (in other words, a reflection of the Existence Absolute in the Power of *māyā*) is called *ekadanta*.

We have seen above the presentation of three *mantras*, the one-syllabled, the eight-syllabled and the *gāyatrī*. In the meditation based on the chanting of the *mantra* of the Personal God, the seeker tries to concentrate either on the sounds of the *mantra* itself or on the form of the Personal God or both. For this reason, it is customary in the scriptures to describe the form of the Lord being worshipped in vivid detail. The vividness helps the seeker to fix the ever vagrant mind on the general description of the Lord (called *dhāraṇā*, a preliminary step for *dhyāna*, the pointed concentration of the mind). Here follows such a vivid description of the Lord's form :

एकदन्तं चतुर्हस्तं पाशमङ्कुशधारिणम् ।

रदं च वरदं हस्तैर्बिभ्राणं मूषकध्वजम् ।।

रक्तं लम्बोदरं शूर्पकर्णकं रक्तवाससम् ।

रक्तगन्धानुलिप्ताङ्गं रक्तपुष्पैस्सुपूजितम् ।।

भक्तानुकम्पिनं देवं जगत्कारणमच्युतम् ।

आविर्भूतं च सृष्ट्यादौ प्रकृतेः पुरुषात्परम् ।

एवं ध्यायति यो नित्यं स योगी योगिनां वरः ।। ११ ।।

ekadantaṁ caturhastaṁ pāśamaṅkuśadhāriṇam ।
radaṁ ca varadaṁ hastairbibhrāṇaṁ mūṣaka-
dhvajam ।।

raktaṁ lambodaraṁ śūrpakarṇakaṁ rakta-
vāsasam ।

raktagandhānuliptāṅgaṁ raktapuṣpaissupū-
jitam ।।

bhaktānukampinaṁ devaṁ jagatkāraṇama-
cyutam ।

āvirbhūtaṁ ca sṛṣṭyādau prakṛteḥ puruṣāt-
param ।

evaṁ dhyāyati yo nityaṁ sa yogī yoginām
varaḥ ।। 11 ।।

The red-hued Lord has one tusk and four
hands. He holds the snare, the goad, and the
tusk in three of His hands, and shows the
boon-bestowing sign with the fingers of the
fourth hand. The symbol on his flag is a mouse.
The Lord with the pot belly has ears like
winnowing baskets. He wears red clothes and
smears red sandal paste to the limbs. He is
worshipped with beautiful red flowers. The
brilliant Lord showers grace on the devotees.
The Lord is the origin of this universe. Yet the

Lord has not fallen down from His innate nature of Existence Absolute in creating this time-bound universe out of Himself. He manifested in this form at the time of creation. He is superior to the Nature and the individual *jīva*. Whosoever contemplates everyday upon the Lord thus is a true seeker; he is the foremost among the devotees.

The Lord's form is generally depicted with four hands. It is a symbolic message to the devotee that he should accomplish the four human goals by the grace of the Lord; they are *dharma* (moderation or righteous action), *artha* (resources or wealth), *kāma* (pursuit of pleasures) and *mokṣa* (liberation from the cycle of birth and death). The Lord has four hands to grant the four desired goals to the devotees. Any form of the Lord, who is essentially formless, is entirely and exclusively meant for the benefit of the devotee. He holds a few weapons in His hands; the idea is that the Lord will drive away evil influences from the life of the devotee. Thus these weapons in the hands of the Lord are meant to reassure the devotee: "O dear devotee, surrender your problems to me and be free." The snare symbolizes ignorance and the Lord alone can liberate the devotee from the hold of delusion. It also signifies time, which is the Power of the Lord. The Lord has absolute control over time. The Lord is timeless, that is, beyond the illusion of time, while the *jīva* (individual) is a prisoner in the circular wall of time.

Whosoever surrenders totally to the Lord will be free from the bondage of the cycle of birth and death. The goad symbolizes that the Lord is in full control of the universe, and the white tusk is meant for destroying the demon of ignorance. Lord Gaṇapati presents his fourth hand before the devotee in a particular *mudrā*. *Mudrā* is a specific

configuration of the fingers signifying a message. It is the
body language of the Lord, since the Lord's form does not
speak. The Lord is assuring the devotee with such a *mudrā*
that his legitimate desires will be fulfilled.

Lord Gaṇapati is presented as red in hue, wearing a
red garment, smeared with red sandal paste, and
worshipped with red flowers. There is a general rule for
the colour of the Lord's form in meditation. If the devotee
seeks knowledge of the Self from the Lord, he may visualize
the Lord as white in complexion. In that case, everything
associated with the form such as the garment, flowers, etc.,
is white. But, when the devotee desires to fulfil certain
legitimate ambitions, he is advised to contemplate on the
red form. The red colour symbolizes the attachment in the
heart of the devotee for the legitimate pleasures of the world,
here and hereafter. Such a devotee prefers red flowers for
worshipping the Lord.

The Lord has a large belly. This is highly symbolic. It is
naive to assume that the Lord is a glutton. The Lord is not
only the origin of this universe, but He also sustains and
protects it, just as a mother protects the child in her womb.
The entire universe has its existence in the Lord. Figuratively
speaking, the universe abides in the large belly of the Lord.
The ears of the Lord resemble the winnowing baskets. Just
as such baskets winnow the chaff from the grains, the Lord
removes the impurity from the mind of the devotee and
makes him eligible for realizing his true nature as non-
different from the Lord.

The Sanskrit verb *div* means brilliance as well as play.
The Lord is the material-cum-efficient cause of this universe.
Creation is a play by the Lord for the Lord in the Lord and
the Lord is the timeless and spaceless Awareness. Since the
universe is only an appearance, and the Lord is its
apparitional cause, there is no real doership or enjoyership

for the Lord with reference to this universe. If the Lord were to be the doer in the absolute sense, that would be a downfall from the exalted position of Existence Absolute, which is timeless. But, though the universe emanating from the Lord is time-bound, the Lord who is the cause of the universe remains timeless. This is the meaning of the word *acyuta*, one who has no downfall.

The one who constantly meditates upon the above form of the Lord is superior to all others. This form of the Lord is very lovable, and people particularly enjoy worshipping or contemplating upon this form.

नमो व्रातपतये । नमो गणपतये । नमः प्रमथपतये । नमस्तेऽस्तु

लम्बोदरायैकदन्ताय विघ्ननाशिने शिवसुताय वरदमूर्तये नमः ।। १२ ।।

namo vrātapataye ı namo gaṇapataye ı namaḥ pramathapataye ı namaste'stu lambodarā- yaikadantāya vighnanāśine śivasutāya varada- mūrtaye namaḥ ıı 12 ıı

My prostrations unto the Lord who is the overlord of all *jīva*s. My prostrations unto the Master of all groups of objects and living beings. My prostrations unto the Head of all the attendants of Lord Śiva. My prostrations unto the One who has a pot belly and a single tusk. My prostrations unto the One who eliminates all obstacles and the One who is the offspring of Lord Śiva. My prostrations unto the Lord's form that is particularly adept at granting boons.

This *mantra* is called the *mālā* (garland) *mantra*, since it is a collection of eight of the most auspicious names of the Lord.

The number eight is auspicious too, since there are eight letters in the Gaṇapati *mahāmantra*. This *mantra* facilitates the communion of the devotee with the Lord. *Vrāta* means an individual, while *gaṇa* is a group. It seems that the devotee says to the Lord : "O Lord, I am the *jīva* and you are the Lord of the *jīvas*. I belong to a family or a group, and you are the Lord of all such groups. The entire universe including me and my group exists, as it were, in your belly. You may remove all the obstacles in our path and grant us boons."

Pramatha literally means the attendant of Lord Śiva, who is capable of destroying the enemies. A devotee who has conquered his base emotions by the strength of devotion to the Lord is the real *pramatha*. The Lord paves the way for such a devotee to realize his identity with Śiva, the *Brahman*, by removing the obstacles caused by ignorance. Lord Gaṇapati is the son of Śiva. But then, the father and the son are One and the same. Śiva is the *nirguṇa Brahman*, while Gaṇapati is the *saguṇa Brahman*. Worship of the latter leads the devotee to gain identity with the former. As already explained, *namaḥ* indicates self-surrender on the part of the devotee. We may say this *namaḥ* with the feeling of surrender any number of times in a day.

Lord Gaṇapati is worshipped by the devotees particularly to eliminate the obstacles in their way. In spite of our best efforts to accomplish any project, there are always hidden factors that may hinder the project. The only way of preventing such hidden barriers is by prayer and worship of Lord Gaṇapati. In the Vedic culture, no auspicious work or ritual is undertaken without first worshipping the Lord Gaṇapati. This worship of the Lord is so common among the followers of Vedic culture that even the annual festivities of the Lord Gaṇapati are started by first worshipping the Lord Gaṇapati.

This concludes the *Ganapati Upaniṣad* proper. What follows is called the *phalaśruti*, a description of various benefits that accrue to the devotee by worshipping the Lord in the form of Gaṇapati. In the Vedic literature, every ritual or mental worship is presented with one or two statements recounting the benefits of such a practice. The object is to motivate the devotee, if such a motivation is required at all. In *niṣkāma karma* (a ritual or prayer performed without a desire for the temporary benefits), the devotee is not interested in material benefits. Yet he gets the highest benefit of communion with the Lord. In some instances, there may be an exaggeration in describing the benefits of the ritual or mental worship. The purpose is only to inspire the seeker on the path of devotion. Such statements are called *arthavāda*, meaning that their spirit alone should be taken into account, ignoring the literal meaning.

एतदथर्वशीर्षं योऽधीते स ब्रह्मभूयाय कल्पते । स सर्वविघ्नैर्न बाध्यते । स सर्वत्र सुखमेधते । स पञ्चमहापापात्प्रमुच्यते । सायमधीयानो दिवसकृतं पापं नाशयति । प्रातरधीयानो रात्रिकृतं पापं नाशयति । सायं प्रातः प्रयुञ्जानो पापोऽपापो भवति । सर्वत्राधीयानोऽपविघ्नो भवति । धर्मार्थकाममोक्षं च विन्दति ॥ १३ ॥

etadatharvaśīrṣaṁ yo'dhīte sa brahmabhūyāya kalpate ι sa sarvavighnairna bādhyate ι sa sarvatra sukhamedhate ι sa pañcamahāpāpāt pramucyate ι sāyamadhīyāno divasakṛtaṁ pāpaṁ nāśayati ι prātaradhīyāno rātrikṛtaṁ pāpaṁ nāśayati ι sāyaṁ prātaḥ prayuñjāno pāpo'pāpo bhavati ι sarvatrādhīyāno'pavighno bhavati ι dharmārtha-kāmamokṣaṁ ca vindati ॥ 13 ॥

Whosoever studies this Upaniṣad of the *Atharvaveda* will realize his oneness with the *Brahman*. He will not encounter any kind of obstacle. He gets absolute happiness at all times, in all places and in all circumstances. He is freed from the five grave sins. By reciting this in the evening, the devotee will be freed from the wrong deeds committed during the day. By reciting this in the morning, he will be freed from the wrong deeds committed during the night. By reciting this both in the evening and in the morning, the devotee will be freed from all his sins and he will become sinless. By reciting this in all situations, the obstacles are eliminated. The devotee will be able to accomplish the four-fold goal of human life : *dharma, artha, kāma* and *mokṣa.*

Here *adhīte* does not mean mechanically reciting the *mantras;* it means knowing the meaning and contemplating on it, and eventually assimilating the truths enunciated in this Upaniṣad. By doing so, the devotee is assured of the highest result possible from spiritual practices, thus getting liberated now and here, even while living in this body. This is not a promise of heaven after death. One can appreciate this process thus. By reciting this Upaniṣad with devotion, the mind of the seeker becomes pure and he or she will attract the infinite grace of the Lord. By this grace the devotee gets a *guru* in his or her life. With the help of the *guru*'s teaching, the person will gain the Self-knowledge which liberates him from the thraldom of *saṁsāra*. There will be no obstacles for him in the path of liberation. The liberated person is happy at all times, in all places and in all circumstances, since he discovers that happiness is his intrinsic nature. He does not require a reason to be happy, unlike others who have to find a reason to be happy. This is indeed the greatest benefit possible.

By reciting this Upaniṣad, all the sins will be washed away. These statements about the removal of sins should be understood in the proper spirit; they should not be taken literally. I knew a vaidika who was mortally afraid of hell after he read a vivid description of the gory scenes of the hell in a Purāṇa. However, he was reassured after listening to this promise of removal of the sins by reciting this Upaniṣad. But, this reassurance went to such an extent that he not only did not repent for his misdeeds, but even developed a cosy feeling that he can also wash away any future sins. Such a literal interpretation of these lines is totally wrong.

That one should recite this Gaṇeśa Upaniṣad both in the morning and evening is presented in a dramatic fashion. It is said quite literally here that by reciting it in the evening, one is absolved of all the wrong deeds committed during the course of the day. On the other hand, if it is recited in the morning, all the mistakes committed in the night are forgiven. This may be understood as meaning that one's heart and mind, and therefore one's actions, become pure if one constantly abides in the thoughts of the Lord. If recited both in the evening and in the morning, one is entirely absolved of all wrongdoing. This assurance implies that one's actions and impulses are purified by this recitation.

Pātayati iti pātakam; an act that pulls down a person is called pātaka. Such an act pushes the agent of that act into the abysmal depths of saṁsāra. In this context, it may be mentioned that the five grave sins are: the extermination of life, eating of the forbidden food like meat, infidelity towards one's life partner, stealing, and revelling in the company of such sinful people. Sometimes gambling is counted as one of the five grave sins. Kings Nala and Dharmarāja, who lost everything in gambling, are good examples. The promise here is that if one recites this Upaniṣad and contemplates upon Gaṇeśa, he will be able to keep away from all kinds of wrong actions.

Some devotees may feel that they are not in a hurry for liberation. They may first be looking for some desired results within *saṁsāra*. Even such devotees will not be disappointed in reciting this Upaniṣad. By the grace of the Lord Gaṇeśa, they will not face obstacles in their chosen path. Again, these statements serve to reemphasize that if one constantly abides in the thoughts of the Lord, all kinds of obstacles can be overcome by His grace.

The scriptures categorize all the endeavours of the entire humanity as directed toward four goals. Every human being desires a few things in life. So, he needs resources to fulfil his desires. These two goals, *kāma* and *artha*, are common to all humans. But, the person's desires must not violate the Natural Law of "live and let live." One's desires and efforts to fulfil them should not clash with those of others. One should not stray away from the path of righteousness while fulfilling the desires. One should not cut corners in acquiring the resources required to fulfil the desires. This is *dharma*, right action or moderation. These three principles of *dharma*, *artha* and *kāma* should define the life of the person in this world. An advanced seeker may eventually like to put an end to the life of seeking. Man is constantly trying to become something other than what he is now. This life of seeking something or the other for being happy has no end. One should realize one's own fullness and blissful nature. This aspiration to realize one's own fullness is called *mokṣa*, which is the ultimate goal of a human being.

These goals can be accomplished by the grace of Lord
Gaṇeśa. In fact, this Upaniṣad is considered to be so
powerful that it can secure all the four goals of life for the
devotee by attracting the grace of the Lord in abundance.

इदमथर्वशीर्षमशिष्याय न देयम् । यो यदि मोहाद्दास्यति स
पापीयान् भवति । सहस्रावर्तनाद्यं यं काममधीते तं तमनेन
साधयेत् ॥ १४ ॥

*idamatharvaśīrṣamaśiṣyāya na deyam । yo yadi
mohāddāsyati sa pāpīyān bhavati। sahasrāvartanādyaṁ yaṁ kāmamadhīte taṁ tamanena
sādhayet ॥ 14 ॥*

This Upaniṣad of the *Atharvaveda* may not be
given to an undeserving disciple. If somebody
does so out of delusion, he is committing a sin.
By reciting this Upaniṣad a thousand times,
one can accomplish any desired end.

There is a mandate that this Upaniṣad may not be taught
to one who is not an eligible student. This is after all a Vedic
mantra and moreover from a very sacred Upaniṣad, and so
it may be taught only to a deserving disciple. Devotion is
an essential qualification for learning this Upaniṣad. A
similar mandate is also given in the *Gītā*. So, if a teacher,
lured by monetary considerations, etc., imparts it to a non-
devotee, he is committing a prohibited act and will invite
adversity. Sometimes even a scholar could fall prey to such
a delusion or greed. The idea here is that this knowledge is
very auspicious and therefore deserves due respect. This
Upaniṣad may be recited numerous times by a devotee who
seeks certain benefits in life. He need not recite the *phalaśruti*
(starting from the 13th *mantra*) every time; it may be recited
only once at the end.

Now, a few rituals based on this Upaniṣad are enjoined
upon the seekers to gain a variety of benefits:

अनेन गणपतिमभिषिञ्चति स वाग्मी भवति । चतुर्थ्यामनश्नन्
जपति स विद्यावान् भवति । इत्यथर्वणवाक्यम् । ब्रह्माद्यावरणं
विद्यान्न बिभेति कदाचनेति ।। १५ ।।

anena gaṇapatimabhiṣiñcati sa vāgmī bhavati ।
caturthyāmanaśnan japati sa vidyāvān bhavati ।
ityatharvaṇavākyam ।   *brahmādyāvaraṇaṁ*
vidyānna bibheti kadācaneti ।। 15 ।।

One who anoints the Lord Gaṇeśa with this
Upaniṣad becomes an orator. One who recites
it throughout the day and fasts on the fourth
day of the lunar calendar becomes a scholar.
This is the promise of the sage Atharvaṇa. By
reciting this till the moment of death, one gains
identity with the *Brahman*, and there remains
no room for fear at any time.

The desire to become an orator or a scholar is laudable.
This scholarship could as well be the knowledge of the Self
which gives liberation. The fourth day of the lunar calendar
(*caturthī*) occurs twice in a month. If a devotee cannot fast
for two days in a month, he may choose the fourth day of
the bright fortnight (in which the moon waxes gradually)
and follow the injunction mentioned herein. If it is not
possible to follow even this injunction, he may do it on the
fourth day in the month of *Bhādrapada*, which is a very
auspicious day for the devotees of the Lord Gaṇeśa. One
who cannot keep total fast for the entire day may do it for
a part of the day. These injunctions and the results thereof
are mandated by the sage Atharvaṇa. This mandate is quite

appropriate since this Upaniṣad belongs to the *Atharvaveda*. The idea is that one may not entertain doubts about the efficacy of the mandate. Human beings live their entire life with insecurity and fear. Fearlessness is indeed *mokṣa*. One who worships the Lord Gaṇeśa by reciting this Upaniṣad lifelong gets that supreme benefit.

यो दूर्वाङ्कुरैर्यजति स वैश्रवणोपमो भवति । यो लाजैर्यजति स यशोवान् भवति । स मेधावान् भवति । यो मोदकसहस्त्रेण यजति स वाञ्छितफलमवाप्नोति । यस्साज्यसमिद्भिर्यजति स सर्वं लभते स सर्वं लभते ।। १६ ।।

yo dūrvāṅkurairyajati sa vaiśravaṇopamo bhavati ı yo lājairyajati sa yaśovān bhavati ı sa medhāvān bhavati ı yo modakasahasreṇa yajati sa vāñchitaphalamavāpnoti ı yassājyasamid-bhiryajati sa sarvaṁ labhate sa sarvaṁ labhate ıı 16 ıı

Whosoever worships the Lord Gaṇeśa with blades of tender grass will gain parity with Kubera; whosoever worships with puffed rice will gain name and fame and also will improve the retentive power of the intellect; whosoever worships with a thousand sweet balls of cooked rice will gain whatever is desired. Whosoever worships the Lord by offering twigs dipped in melted butter certainly gains everything.

Tender blades of grass are routinely used in pairs for worshipping the Lord Gaṇeśa, while reciting this Upaniṣad or while chanting His hundred or thousand names. Such a

worshipper gains plenty of wealth, so much so he gains
parity with Kubera, the divine treasurer of the universe.
Puffed rice is used in Vedic rituals as an offering in the fire
to the gods. It is considered an auspicious material like
turmeric. Hindus believe that sweet balls of cooked rice are
particularly favoured by the Lord Gaṇeśa. In fire oblations,
the twigs of the peepul tree are normally used. Sometimes,
even the twigs of a mango tree can be used in the absence
of a peepul tree. These twigs are to be gathered off the
ground where they fall from a dry branch. This fire oblation
is routinely performed by *vaidika*s even now. The message
conveyed by these promises of the Upaniṣad is that the
devotee will gain the grace of the Lord in abundance.

Reciting this Upaniṣad a thousand times with devotion
becomes a *puraścaraṇa*. Devotees take a vow to recite it a
thousand times and then finish it in a specified time. This
vow is called *puraścaraṇa*, because it is supposed to be the
first priority in the devotee's life (*puraḥ prathamam caryate
iti*).

अष्टौ ब्राह्मणान् सम्यग् ग्राहयित्वा सूर्यवर्चस्वी भवति । सूर्यग्रहे महानद्यां
प्रतिमासन्निधौ वा जप्त्वा सिद्धमन्त्रो भवति । महाविघ्नात् प्रमुच्यते ।
महादोषात् प्रमुच्यते । महाप्रत्यवायात् प्रमुच्यते । स सर्वविद् भवति स
सर्वविद् भवति । य एवं वेद । इत्युपनिषत् ।। १७ ।।

ओं शान्तिश्शान्तिश्शान्तिः ।।

*aṣṭau brāhmaṇān samyag grāhayitvā
sūryavarcasvī bhavati ı sūryagrahe
mahānadyāṁ pratimāsannidhau vā japtvā
siddhamantro bhavati ı mahāvighnāt
pramucyate ı mahādoṣāt pramucyate ı
mahāpratyavāyāt pramucyate ı sa sarvavid*

bhavati sa sarvavid bhavati ı ya evaṁ veda,
ityupaniṣat ıı 17 ıı

ोṁ *śāntiśśāntiśśāntiḥ* ıı

One who teaches this Upaniṣad to eight Vedic
scholars becomes as brilliant as the sun. At the
time of solar eclipse, the devotee may recite
this on the bank of a great river or recite this
in front of an idol of Lord Gaṇeśa in front of
him. By doing so, the devotee will get all the
benefits of this *mantra*. He will be freed from
the most major obstacle, from the most major
blemish and from the most major wrongdoing. Whosoever worships the Lord thus,
becomes omniscient, — becomes omniscient.
om, peace, peace, peace.

The number eight is significant, since there are eight letters
in the great *mantra* of the Lord Gaṇeśa. One who teaches
this to eight deserving devotees would gain a lustre such as
that of the sun. In India·during the solar or lunar eclipse
people go to a river, bathe, stand in the water and pray.
Food is avoided and no other activity is performed during
the eclipse. It is the time for prayer and prayer alone;
nothing else. So, that particular time is recommended for
chanting this Upaniṣad, because there is a special power in
the prayer during such a special astronomical event.

The big obstacle for the devotee is *saṁsāra*, the world-
centric life. One cannot but be in the world, but should not
be of the world. It is not easy to overcome the world-bound
outlook, which is so deeply ingrained in our psyche. We
need all the grace of the Lord to become less passionate
about the things of the world. The major blemish on the

part of a human being is the absence of the Self-knowledge. *Pratyavāya* is also an obstacle, but of the intrinsic kind like a strong orientation towards sinfulness. All obstacles to Self-knowledge will be removed when this Upaniṣad is repeatedly chanted.

Whosoever meditates upon the Lord through this Upaniṣad becomes omniscient. There is only one way of knowing all and that is by knowing the One. In the vision of Vedānta, it is well established that by knowing *Brahman* as *ātman*, everything else is effectively known, since everything exists and shines in the Awareness Absolute, which is the *ātman*.

Repetition of the last statement twice is the indication that the Upaniṣad ends here. Thus the Upaniṣad concludes with the promise of Self-knowledge to the devotee of Lord Gaṇeśa. Upaniṣad means a secret. It is a secret in the sense that only an eligible devotee may be initiated into it.

।। हरिः ओम्, तत्सत्, श्रीकृष्णार्पणमस्तु ।।

।। *hariḥ oṁ, tatsat, śrīkṛṣṇārpaṇamastu* ।।

Index